Market
YOURSELF
and Your
CAREER

Market
YOURSELF
and Your
CAREER

JEFF DAVIDSON MBA CMC

Adams Media Corporation
Holbrook, Massachusetts

DEDICATION

To high achievers everywhere.

Published by
Adams Media Corporation
260 Center Street, Holbrook, MA 02343

ISBN: 1-58062-119-8

Printed in the United States of America.
J I H G F E D C B A

Library of Congress Cataloging-in-Publication Data

Davidson, Jeffrey P.
Market yourself and your career / by Jeff Davidson
p. cm.
Rev. ed. of: Blow your own horn: how to market
yourself and your career. ©1987.
Includes index.
ISBN 1-58062-119-8
1. Career development. 2. Professions—Marketing. 3. Success in business.
I. Davidson, Jeffrey P. Blow your own horn. II. Title.
HF5381.D297   1999
650.14—dc221   99-20339
CIP

This book is available at quantity discounts for bulk purchases.
For information, call 1-800-872-5627
(in Massachusetts, 781-767-8100).

Visit our home page at http://www.adamsmedia.com

CONTENTS

ACKNOWLEDGMENTS

MANY PEOPLE HELPED IN THE PREPARATION OF this book. Diane Walbrecker and Katherine Reynolds made key conceptual and editorial contributions. Seth Kotch, Anna Hayes, and Kate Simpson helped in editing and proofing.

Thanks to Ed Walters, whose enthusiasm for the project made it a "go," and Wayne Jackson for his astute marketing input and support. Thanks to Carrie Lewis in Promotions, Nancy True in Subsidiary Rights. Thanks most of all to Bob Adams for his constant vision and excellence.

Thanks also to subject matter experts Margaret Bedrosian, Lou Hampton, Janet G. Elsea, Ph.D., Tony Alessandra, Ph.D., Dr. Harry Olson, Jim Cathcart, Dr. Donald Moine, Robert Bookman, David and Ann Murphy Springer, Lyman Steil, Ph.D., Brian Jud, Robert Goldstein, Ph.D., Chester L. Karrass, Ph.D., Richard Cupka, Andrew Dyke, Ph.D., Jefferson Bates, Bert Decker, Ph.D., Fran Campbell, Joe Stumpf, David McClelland, Ph.D., Marcia Yudkin, Sam Horn, Roger Herman, Joyce Degioia, Arnold "Nick" Carter, and Terry Paulson, Ph.D. for their ideas, support, or contributions to specific chapters.

Thanks also to Sandy Knudsen for her consistently excellent word processing support, and Valerie Davidson, age 8, for her supreme wisdom, inspiration, and patience.

FOREWORD

WHEN I FIRST CAME TO THIS COUNTRY FROM England in 1962, corporate America looked a great deal different than it does today. Needing to find work quickly to replenish my rapidly dwindling resources, I went to work as a trainee for the Bank of America, then the largest bank in the world even though it only had branches in California. I looked forward to a long career with them. I was willing to put in a solid eight hours a day, five days a week (minus, of course, one or two state or federal holidays a month). I could expect periodic performance reviews, promotions, and raises in pay. How different than today's corporate environment!

Today, unrelenting, ever-increasing worldwide competition has placed enormous pressure on all corporate employees, from the chairman of the board all the way down to newly hired workers. Information overload is putting pressure on executives and managers in all organizations, and a "lean and mean" mentality has pervaded all levels of business. Increasingly business leaders and managers are being asked to accomplish more and more, with fewer and fewer resources.

Consider the impact of all this on your boss. When you understand the pressure that he or she is under, it's easy to understand why (despite your yeoman efforts) you may not be getting the rewards and recognition you feel you deserve.

As Jeff Davidson so eloquently explains in this great book, the era is long gone when merely doing a good job would get you where you wanted to go in your career. To be a savvy career achiever in today's world, you need to develop and implement a specific plan of action that will get you noticed and moving ahead at your company. That's what Jeff Davidson's *Market Yourself and Your Career* will do for you. I think that it will be the most important career-advancing book you'll ever read.

Market Yourself and Your Career was originally published some twelve years ago as *Blow Your Own Horn*. Berkeley Books went on to publish the book in mass market and Simon & Schuster created an audiocassette which has sold 52,400 copies, and is still selling well. The original book was also selected by the Prentice-Hall and McGraw Hill book clubs, and published in several languages. In short, you've got a classic in your hands. This version is completely revised and updated.

Jeff lays out a comprehensive approach to ensure that you will: progress in your career, generate visibility both within your organization and in your industry, and increase your career skills. He tackles many issues not addressed in other books, such as: why it's important to work harder when your boss is away, why it's vital to make allies out of the clerical and production staff, and why it's wise to take on the job or task that no one else in your department or division wants to tackle.

One thing that I love about the book is the way that it's structured. Jeff assumes that you are already extremely busy, and the last thing you need is a whole new set of tasks on top of those you're currently juggling. So he's structured this book so that you can use what he calls "piggybacking principles." He'll teach you how to use leverage to get more mileage out of what you're already doing. The techniques you'll learn have worked for tens of thousands of career achievers, and they will work for you as well.

The 21 chapters that follow offer you a sequential plan to effectively market your career and yourself, without feeling that you've taken on a second job. You'll explore which outside groups and organizations will best further your career. You'll learn the nuances of getting articles published, or getting mentioned in articles written by others. You'll learn the important elements of giving an effective speech, and why it's essential to engage in public speaking to groups in your community. You'll learn the importance of keeping an internal achievement list that you can refer to at opportune moments. You'll learn how to identify the ten key people you need to know to keep your career trajectory on an upward path, and why that's vital to your career. You'll also learn who gets ahead and why, how to generate visibility for both yourself and your organization, and how to continually prime the pump so as to make the best of every situation and assignment.

You're in for an adventure, unlike any you've encountered with other career-related books. The chapter on becoming indispensable alone offers a veritable gold mine of ideas for becoming a highly valued member of your organization, no matter how long you've been there, and no matter what your position.

Think about all the projects that you've successfully completed, the reports that you've turned in on time, and the customers you've handled with grace and ease. If you've suspected that there must be ways to harness all of the hard work that you've done so that you're continually assured of being noticed, recognized, and rewarded, then your ship has come in. *Market Yourself and Your Career* will give you the career edge that you desire and deserve.

—Roger Dawson, author of
Roger Dawson's Secrets of Power Negotiating.

MARKETING YOUR CAREER

I S SELF-MARKETING NECESSARY? IF I'M BRIGHT, ambitious, and hardworking, won't I rise to the top of my career ladder without any special marketing effort? Increasingly, the answer to the last question is no. Those in the baby boom generation, born between 1946 and the early '60s, are part of the largest "generational cohort" in history. As a result, they've been up against significant competition at every stage of their lives—getting into a good college, finding that first job, locating an affordable apartment, meeting the right mate, and so on.

Like the baby boomers, the Generation Xers, those born between the early '60s and early '80s, have faced a rapidly changing, uncertain business environment dominated by managers that sometimes don't understand them, or the special capabilities and insights they have to offer.

Under the circumstances, maintaining a competitive advantage isn't merely a good idea—it's a necessity. And self-marketing is a vital part of that effort.

This book acknowledges and explores the notions that you need to be your own career coach; that career marketing is a continual process; that the continued development of interpersonal skills supports career advancement; and that, for many people, professional exposure is the fastest ticket to the top.

AT THE HELM OF YOUR OWN CAREER

Where is the locus of control for your career? Is it your boss, your parents, the government, your spouse, your peers? Realistically, you and you alone are in control of your career. Frequently, people tell me how a difficult boss held them back, how they simply didn't have time to write an article, or how they "have never been effective" at networking. Such statements only shift the blame for not reaching career goals onto others or "inherent" traits.

You certainly can be the victim of a bad organization or a bad boss, and in the short run, there are good reasons why you couldn't take the proactive step that would help propel your career. In the long run, however, there aren't any excuses. You're in control of your career; it doesn't control you.

SET GOALS EARLY FOR THE GREATEST IMPACT

Generally, the earlier you set goals, make a commitment, and take action, the greater the long-term results. Yet there's no use in bemoaning the fact that you didn't set goals previously, or that you wasted the last few years in a dead-end job. *Today* is the future you were thinking about three years ago. That time has come and gone. Will what you're doing three years from now be supported by action that you initiate today?

Contemporary society, unfortunately, propels us faster and faster toward immediate gratification. Long-term planning, sacrifice, and patience seem rare among the masses who have been programmed to have it all, do it all, and to have it and do it all *now*. The article you write next week, however, may not be accepted for another couple of months and may not be published until a year from now. The groups you call about a speaking engagement may not return your call for several weeks or months, and may not schedule a date until the middle of next year.

Few of the career marketing activities discussed in this book offer spectacular, immediate payoffs (although some of them definitely do). Successful career marketers realize that careers last many years, indeed decades, and that you have to balance short- and long-term activities to take care of what has to be done today and to support what you choose to do tomorrow.

Career professionals who recognize the one-to-one ratio of effort and accomplishment view their careers not simply in terms of today, next week, or next year, but as a long, unfolding journey. These professionals have a definite edge over the rest.

Sharon Louise Connelly Ph.D., in her dissertation, "Work Spirit: Recapturing the Vitality of Work," observed that "individuals demonstrating work spirit have a sense that everything that they have ever done contributes to what they are working toward."

ACKNOWLEDGING WHAT EXISTS

The more closely we can manage our careers in accordance with reality, the greater the return for our efforts. The late, great motivational speaker Earl Nightingale said, "It is easier to adjust ourselves to the hardships of a poor living than it is to adjust ourselves to the hardships of making a better one." This reality applies to individuals, communities, regions, and even entire countries. It also helps explain why, when we attempt to move from where we are, often we end up settling for where we started from.

My own tendency to "accept the hardship of a poor living" was brought home to me after I won a large and prestigious consulting contract several years ago. My deputy project manager and I plotted 109 steps for successfully completing the project. This planning session required our full time and attention for two days. At the end of this process, we had created a plan that we knew down to the marrow in our bones would work and serve us well. Thereafter, I realized the value of applying the same time and energy to plot the steps required to advance my career. Nevertheless, I didn't get started for three years. I am pleased to say, however, that I made up for lost time!

If you don't set goals, and you don't pursue them vigorously, no one else will be keeping score; maybe you can continue to get by. In those quiet moments, however, when there's no one to answer to but ourselves, how do we justify procrastinating for years? How do we justify not making the effort to achieve what we want to achieve?

For the vast majority of us, barring outrageous misfortune, life is a self-fulfilling prophesy, and playing it safe, not taking a risk, not going the extra mile, or accepting the hardship of a poor living becomes our fate. The longer we stay in that mode, the harder it is to get out. The way out is through *action*.

TAKING ACTION: CAREER MARKETER

In many ways, marketing is life. Often, those who get ahead in life are natural-born marketers. Elected politicians, your organization's top executive, and all those people society respects somehow mastered the ability to effectively and visibly serve a constituency, shareholders, or other target group.

Whether you were a marketing major in college or have never read one word on the topic, you can become an effective career marketer. Implementing the strategies and recommendations in this book requires no particular marketing background or aptitude. What's required is the ability to produce a self-definition, set goals to which you are committed, and pursue your goals vigorously.

An important note: To become an effective career marketer doesn't mean being boastful, arrogant, pushy, or egotistical; it doesn't mean using other people or employing deceit or trickery. As you'll learn in this book, the most effective self-marketing is done with class and honesty, and is based on a genuine respect and concern for the needs of others. As marketing professionals will tell you, without a worthwhile product or service, no amount of puffery can produce long-term results. It's the same with career marketing. The secret is simply to develop the skills that will make you a valuable professional, and then learn to promote those skills so as to earn the respect and success you deserve.

Each of the following chapters is based on my personal experience, including failures and successes, in marketing my own career.

What I'm presenting has actually worked for me, and, if aggressively implemented, will work for you as well.

Jeff Davidson
Chapel Hill, North Carolina
May 1999

PART I

STEERING YOUR CAREER

YOUR PERSONAL MARKETING PLAN

. . . I am the master of my fate and the captain of my soul.

—Invictus

WHO NEEDS A MARKETING PLAN? For one, you do. You need a marketing plan to sell products, services, ideas, and above all, yourself. A concise marketing plan will allow you to focus your time and energy in one direction, thereby increasing your effectiveness. It defines what you're offering, to whom, and through what methods. Without a marketing plan, you're likely to keep jousting at windmills.

Your marketing plan is an organized, written tool describing your present career situation, opportunities, and problems, and establishing specific and realistic career goals. It also outlines specific action steps required to accomplish these goals, including a milestone chart.

As a strategic career marketer, one of your chief responsibilities is anticipating changes that will allow you time to act decisively. Since your plan needs to change as you and your environment change, career marketing planning is a continual process. Let's look at the simplest marketing plan that'll get you started and how it works!

YOUR OWN ONE-MINUTE DEFINITION

Develop a one-sentence, one-minute definition of what you have to offer or want to offer to the world—a one-sentence "marketing plan." That one sentence, carefully developed, will point you in the right direction and help focus all your efforts.

This is my own sentence:

I'm in the business of inspiring and educating career professionals everywhere to *live and work at a comfortable pace* in our sped-up world, and to provide unique resources in the form of books, audio-video, software, online support, and speaking engagements that help people meet tough daily challenges.

That one (long!) sentence describes the services I provide, for whom, and how. As time passes, undoubtedly I'll revise it.

As a career professional, your one-sentence marketing definition needs to be realistic, acknowledging your current position and focusing on the future. After establishing your one key sentence, you can turn your attention to setting—and reaching—your goals.

Setting and Reaching Goals

I set goals before dinner, on planes, even when I am not planning to do it. The process of goal setting involves some initial overreaching then sifting through to find the realistic, attainable gems.

When is the best time to pick goals? Whenever they pop up. Or, to put it more scientifically, when you're in a relaxed, creative, contemplative state of mind. The early twentieth century author Napoleon Hill once said that "imagination is the workshop of the mind." Open up your mind to the full range of possibilities.

LET IMAGINATION RULE

One of the most effective ways to achieve your goals is to marshal the power of your imagination. Suppose your goal is to succeed at an important business meeting or forthcoming event. One approach is using visualization, a technique whose success has been documented in the now-classic book, *Psychocybernetics*, by Maxwell Maltz. Here's how to use the technique:

- Sit back in your chair, take a deep breath, relax, and allow your eyes to close. To help yourself relax, focus your attention on your breath, noticing how you inhale and exhale. Simply take note of it, without trying to change anything about the way you're breathing.

- Now, recall scenes from favorite movies, or how your parents looked the last time you saw them. Use this same technique of visualization to picture the meeting or event concerning you.

- In your imagination, see who is at this meeting. Notice what you and the others are wearing and the meeting location. Is it in your office? In a restaurant? If so, what are people eating or drinking?

- What would you like to hear people saying to you in this meeting? What is the ideal outcome?

- Imagine people saying exactly what you would like to hear them say. Imagine representing yourself with all the confidence, poise, wisdom, knowledge, and persuasiveness you'd like to convey.

- Use as many of your senses—sight, hearing, touch, taste, and smell—as you can to make the scene as real as possible.

Visualization often takes time to emerge and grow. What you visualize may seem sketchy the first few times you try, but stay with it. Watch how it develops as you define more clearly exactly what you want.

It's useful to practice visualization for short-term goals throughout the day, especially if you find yourself worried about a particular issue. When the worry pops up, substitute your positive visualization for the negative worry.

Visualize your ideal career each morning before getting out of bed and each night before going to bed. During the day, if you start to worry while you're busy, instead of undertaking the whole visualization, substitute a picture and the feeling of pure white light for worry. This can positively redirect the negative focus of your worry.

You can use visualization for other short-term and long-term goals, including those involving money, employee relationships, proposals you have to write, family situations . . . anything that concerns you. Simply "see," "hear," and "experience" the perfect outcome in your imagination.

READY, FIRE, AIM

Reaching goals requires focusing on them and taking appropriate action. Tom Peters and Robert Waterman, authors of the 1980s bestseller, *In Search of Excellence*, observed that for many years, businesses were stuck in the "ready, aim, fire" mode. The first step in any new project, "ready," was to gather reams of data, and then analyze, assess, and evaluate what needed to be done. Next came "aim"—careful planning, test marketing, or simulation—followed by "fire"—actually getting started on the project.

You can use a different concept—ready, fire, aim—in planning your career. This idea, discussed by Peters and Waterman, involves making a *brief* assessment of your skills and the career direction you anticipate, followed by an early "firing," or getting into the actual activity quickly. The "aim," which involves readjusting, modifying, or honing career plans, is the final task.

Let's look at an example. Gerard works for the human resources division of a large manufacturing company. He's compiled some data which revealed graphically that to reach his financial or long-term advancement goals, he'd have to move from his current job.

Gerard checks the salary ranges in his company and compares the position descriptions with his skills and abilities. The best match he comes across is a position in the marketing department.

Rather than evaluating any further, Gerard joins the local chapter of the American Marketing Association, has lunch separately with three of the marketers currently in the division, and plants a bug in the ear of the vice president of marketing about wanting a career change.

Gerard has made a series of quick moves and has taken control of the situation. Later, if he discovers disadvantages to joining the marketing department, he can reexamine his plan.

The "ready, fire, aim" concept helps you start full-scale activities immediately while minimizing wasted time and energy. It gives you a chance to make small mistakes in your career path and quickly retreat from them.

MILESTONES KEEP YOU FOCUSED

Establishing milestones for the realization of the career goals you've chosen is essential. Start with a list of possible career goals. Your list might include goals like these:

- To earn $1 million in ten years.
- To be transferred to the Singapore division of the company.
- To be featured in the company newsletter and online 'zine.
- To be mentioned in *Forbes* magazine.
- To publish a book.

Chances are that no two people will have exactly the same goals. Based on your own list, prepare a milestone chart (see Figure 1-1) showing when you plan to accomplish each of your goals. There are many varieties of software—database, project management, spreadsheet and word processing—available to aid your efforts. This is a convenient way to maintain command of the timing and progress toward your established goals.

Your milestone chart could delineate each goal and subgoal, including starting time, anticipated ending time, and a schedule or subgoals—you can load it up with interim dates to aid in your progress and overall planning.

FIGURE 1-1, MILESTONE CHART

Goal	Year One	Year Two	Year Three
Meet five marketing directors	⊢—⊣		
Write article	⊢—⊣		
Increase salary to 65K	⊢—⊣		
Appear on three radio talk shows	⊢—⊣	⊢—⊣	⊢—⊣
Write first book	⊢———————⊣		
Be featured in my industry's major journal		⊢———⊣	
Be promoted to department manager		⊢———⊣	
Attend special executive development program		⊢—⊣	
Increase salary to 75K			⊢—⊣
Write second book			⊢———⊣

Let's say that you have set the goal of making the acquaintance of five marketing directors from other companies in your field. You wish to accomplish this through attending meetings and writing letters with follow-up telephone calls within the next six months. On your milestone chart, you would plot this six-month period and follow through. Unlike the would-be dieter who is always going to start next week, your campaign begins the moment your milestone chart calls for commencing the activity plotted. If you want to change your milestone chart, of course, that's fine, but don't fool around with your goals—if you set them, intend to reach them.

If the task or activity is something that you've never undertaken before, such as writing articles for exposure, be generous in allocating time for its accomplishment. A common weakness of many capable people is to unrealistically estimate the time it will take to accomplish something. By adding a safety margin, the probability of reaching your goal is greater.

A goal you set two months or two years ago may be inappropriate today because of changes brought about by reaching other goals, changes in your home life, or changes in the external environment; so it's vital to fine-tune your goals on a regular basis.

COMMITMENT IS THE CAPPER

The key to effective goal setting is commitment, without which no doors will open for you and none of life's treasure chests will be unlocked. "I think true overnight successes are extremely rare," states mega-author Herman Holtz. "Successes may come suddenly and swiftly, after a lengthy struggle, but that lengthy struggle is almost always the prior necessity." Once you've chosen your goals and established some milestones, you owe it to yourself to make the effort. Don't build yourself up by listing, visualizing, and preparing goals without fully dedicating yourself to achieving them.

Setting career goals will not guarantee success, but evidence strongly supports the theory that goal attainment is far more likely if those goals are clearly identified and serve as a focus.

Goal setting is the first and most important step you can take on your career marketing path. The following chapters introduce and discuss various strategies, techniques, and tools to market your career and help you attain your goals.

CHAPTER 2

MANAGING YOUR TIME TO MARKET YOUR CAREER

If you're too busy to enjoy your life, you're way too busy.

—Jeff Davidson

O VER THE YEARS, I'VE SPOKEN TO HUNDREDS OF groups and thousands of individuals on career marketing. Many are motivated to achieve their goals, and a large number already possess the requisite skills. However, the one thing everyone seems to say is that they don't have enough time. Write an article? Prepare a speech? Who's got time? Perhaps there is no greater obstacle to effective career marketing than managing one's time.

Here's the ten million dollar lotto jackpot of a question: Is there enough time to do your job, market your career, and otherwise lead a balanced life? Yes, there is. This chapter addresses fundamental—and more elaborate—aspects of time and self-management so that you will be able to do your job and act on the advice in following chapters to market your career.

CARVING IT OUT

"Most people think time management is defined by the little rules we employ to stay organized such as touch a piece of paper only once, or write everything down, or always call ahead to confirm an appointment. In my view, that's micro-management (and certainly important)," says Mark McCormack, author of *What They Don't Teach You at Harvard Business School.*

"It's also important to step back and look at the areas where you're spending big chunks of time every day. It's no good being a role model of split-second efficiency if you're working on the wrong things," he says. "A well organized person reviews the calendar as well as the clock and focuses on key areas: personal time - the most important thing you have to do is allow time for your family and personal relationships. This should be everyone's number one priority, but a lot of people get it backward. They block out time for family and friends only *after* their work is out of their way. Actually, it should be the other way around; first fix a percentage of time for family, then use the remaining time for everyone else," says McCormack.

MAKING WORK COUNT TWICE

The time you have available undoubtedly has to be allocated wisely, as McCormack says, over a number of choices. How can you manage your time, however, when faced with increasing demands in all areas?

Early in my career I gravitated to the notion of making my work count twice. For example, at the end of each consulting engagement, I had to prepare a report. From many of the reports I was able to extract passages that could be converted into articles that were later published. Many of those articles were used again in books as chapters or parts of chapters, such as this one.

The same technique can be applied to other kinds of work. The key after completing any task is to ask yourself whether the results can be used in any other way—to solve a different problem, meet someone else's need, or create a new and profitable way to proceed. Once you get into the habit of seeking to make your work count twice, you'll be surprised at how effective it can be.

KNOW WHERE THE TIME GOES

Recognizing where your time is wasted is a good way to give yourself more time for career marketing. If you do too many simple tasks yourself rather than delegating them to your subordinates, the obvious solution is to delegate more. A list of guidelines to help you manage telephone time, such as the example in Figure 2-1 later in this chapter, can be modified for meetings or any of your other activities.

Another excellent way to make time for things you consider important is to learn to say, "No!" How many of us end up doing things we feel only mildly interested in because we haven't learned to say "No"? That word, which requires practice, needs to be couched in something positive. For instance, if someone asks you to review a paper, say, "I'd like to, but I'm pressed for time right now, so I'll have to pass."

If you find yourself having trouble saying "No" to unwanted social obligations or business commitments that distract you from your major goals, create a mental picture of yourself overcoming the distraction. One author taped the word "no" on her telephone to help her turn down lectures and requests for writing advice that become destructive to her own time.

Be ruthless in avoiding time wasters and stick to your plan of target dates and priorities. Select your priorities carefully. Make sure you do not let anything interfere with your plans for a certain segment of time.

Be careful with your time when you're "on a roll." Don't let anything interrupt you if you are feeling highly productive. Lock the door, unplug the phone, do whatever it takes to maintain the momentum. Tape-record meetings if you can't take notes fast enough.

Also, invest in time-saving devices. Any piece of equipment that pays for itself in a year is worth it. My friend Bill let years pass without plunking down $200 to secure an item that would double his productivity. He felt that "the organization should pay for it." What a career loss!

GO TO COLLEGE DURING TRAVEL TIME

The average American commutes 157,589 miles to work during his or her lifetime, the equivalent of traveling six times around the world, and that's not counting the added time and gasoline consumed in stop-and-go traffic. Think of the staggering proportion of commuting time that you spend sitting in traffic jams—and then plan some ways to use that time productively.

Install a cassette player in your car. Tapes are now available for such items as management and business books, classic novels, and old radio shows. Slip some extra reading material into your car also. Those minutes and hours spent sitting in unavoidable traffic can be used wisely.

If you travel by air to any of the hub cities, such as New York, Detroit, Chicago, Dallas, or Atlanta, you will almost surely spend some time you didn't anticipate on the runway or in the terminal. Similar to installing a cassette player or CD player and carrying extra reading material in your car for everyday use, be prepared while you're traveling. Bring the stack of items you've wanted to complete and if your trip is longer than three days, mail the package back to yourself. Maybe you won't get to use the time, but there's nothing so frustrating as not having anything to do.

Get Organized—Save Time

Unquestionably, getting and staying organized takes time and thought, but it saves even more time than it takes, while at the same time offering peace of mind. Why not view getting organized as preparation time "to respond to life?" Knowing where things are—

papers you need for a report, backup supplies, important phone numbers and addresses—gives you the freedom to concentrate on creative, more fulfilling work.

Save time by making up address labels for people to whom you write frequently. Use return addresses as labels for your next correspondence with that person. Think of the time you spend running to the post office because you used the 20 stamps you bought last week. Buy a roll of 100 stamps at a time; you'll most likely need them. The same advice holds true for any supply you use often.

PALM TOPS AND POCKET ORGANIZERS

A wide assortment of palm tops and electronic organizers are available today. These devices enable you to store names and addresses, keep appointments on your calendar, record notes, maintain lists, and, in general, help keep your career on a progressive plane. Such devices can help you identify scheduling conflicts, search through thousands of records to quickly find the contact person or information you need, and personalize the way you search and retrieve records.

You can print your calendar or key lists of addresses in hard copy to take with you. You can toggle on alarms and buzzers to serve as reminders for when to make a call. You can even have the call dialed for you. Electronic organizers enable you to insert icons both on appointment calendars and lists you're maintaining. Icons could include a flower, a football, the moon, stars, an ice skate, or a book, among many others.

Most electronic organizers assist you by automatically completing some fields in your address book when it recognizes keystrokes. So, if you start to type the letters "Ral," it will complete the entire name of the city, "Raleigh," without your having to type the rest.

As prices keep dropping and the almighty chip gets more power, if you don't already have an electronic organizer, you likely will, soon enough.

IT'S A PERSONAL THING

Organization is individual, uniquely you. A desk or office that would drive you mad may seem perfectly organized to a coworker. Keeping yourself comfortably organized will reduce your stress, increase your productivity, and often influence others to view you as a competent professional.

Establish your files in advance. Having the items you need on hand will lower your frustration level.

Getting organized affords a sense of control over your life, rather than having your life control you. This sense of well-being will spread into other areas of your life.

Why is the *perception* that you're organized important in your career marketing effort? Organized people are viewed, rightly or not, as more capable than disorganized people. The impression you create by being in control adds points in your favor.

A QUICK QUIZ: HOW ORGANIZED ARE YOU?

1. Is your desk at work or at home piled horizontally with reports, papers, and files? Nobody can manage a horizontal pile.
2. Do you have trouble finding a particular item in your desk that you use often? Maybe it needs to be left *on* your desk.
3. Do you feel that you could be organized if you only had more space? More space is seldom the answer; filing or getting rid of what isn't important often is.
4. Do you have piles of newspapers and magazines at home that you don't have time to read? If you're attempting to read these publications cover to cover, good luck. Clip out what looks important or interesting, and chuck the rest.
5. Do papers clutter your desk for at least a week? A desk is not a filing cabinet.

6. Do you ever find something at the bottom of a pile that you didn't know was there? Beware: you're liable to lose anything! Break down your piles now.

7. Do you sometimes spend five to ten minutes or more looking for a letter or document that you need? The search should take no more than 45 to 75 seconds. More than that and you're wasting everyone's time.

8. Do you read every piece of unsolicited or junk mail that crosses your desk? Most of this mail can be discarded at once. Take but a few seconds to determine whether to keep, route, or throw out junk mail.

MAKING THE MOST OF YOUR TIME ON THE PHONE

By using the charts in Figure 2-1, adapted from those developed by management consultants David and Ann Murphy Springer, you can identify telephone time thieves. Simply log every incoming and outgoing call for 7 to 10 days or until you see a pattern.

MANAGING YOUR PRODUCTIVITY CYCLE

Everyone has productive peaks and valleys throughout the course of the normal work week—periods of higher and lower energy and creativity. This pattern makes up your own *cycle of productivity*. For all but urgent assignments, handle assignments on those days and at those hours that achieve a relatively constant "effort-to-task" ratio.

Productive people who are able to pace themselves accomplish more in less time and remain more vibrant. They have an internal "time grid" that charts their cycle of productivity, even though no formal sketch or chart is ever made. Don't avoid telling your supervisor that you'd "rather not handle the DEF report right now" because you "can do a better job on it tomorrow morning," and the "GHI assignment is best undertaken now." If neither report reprsents an emergency, your schedule should prevail.

FIGURE 2-1, IDENTIFYING TELEPHONE TIME THIEVES

Telephone Time Manager—Outgoing Calls

To _____ Date _____

Is this call necessary? _____

What priority is it? _____

Is an agenda prepared? _____

Are notes and info at hand? _____

Is this the right time to call? _____

Can other issues be handled? _____

Was chatting minimized? _____

Was the issue resolved? _____

Person was unavailable/no answer/I left message _____

Recipient didn't have info _____

I was redirected to another person _____

Further action needed _____

Target Time _____

Actual Time _____

Telephone Time Manager—Incoming Calls

From _____ Date _____

Is this call necessary ? _____

Could someone else have effectively handled the caller? ____

Was a subordinate seeking info that he or she could have
    gotten elsewhere? _____

Did I get the info I wanted? _____

Was the issue resolved? _____

Was a decision made? _____

Do I know what further action I need to take? _____

Did I minimize chatting? _____

Target Time _____

Actual Time _____

Given that you're already a highly productive employee, there are four basic ways to get the most from yourself by working in sync with your cycle of productivity.

1. Ask for enough assignments so that the cycle can be used. If you have only one task, obviously there is little leeway in undertaking that task at the most personally opportune time. With many assignments, however, you can strategically arrange your schedule.

2. Seek flexibility in due dates. You know you'll productively finish the important jobs on time. You can finish assignments of lesser importance as soon as possible. The more flexibility you're afforded in completing assignments, the greater the opportunity for you to execute assignments in accordance with the cycle. So, next time you're assigned a particular project, find out when it has to be done or if it could be done following something else. More often than not, given a flexible due date, you'll complete many assignments sooner than you anticipated.

3. Coordinate with your boss to avoid late afternoon and surprise assignments. As a productive employee, in concurrence with your cycle of productivity, you intuitively allocate tasks for the late afternoon. Frequent late afternoon surprise assignments mess up your cycle.

4. Closely related to the above, seek advance notice of assignments. The more notice you have, the better you'll be able to schedule the new assignment in accordance with your cycle of productivity.

"Concentrated" Career Marketing

Concentration is the ability to focus attention voluntarily, to ignore irrelevant proceedings, and to fix power and effort to a single goal. Concentration is a time management tool that you can increase through practice.

Distractions abound. If you're looking for reasons *not* to get a job done or *not* to concentrate on a task, plenty exist. In fact, anything can become a distraction to your concentration if you allow it to interfere. Distractions dissipate your energy level and reduce your productivity with a resulting increase in your level of stress.

To increase your power of concentration, eliminate outside distractions! Taking control of your environment increases your confidence and enhances your career marketing efforts. You're in charge, not those who call you on the telephone or otherwise fritter away your time.

HOLD THE CALLS

To what degree you can, hold calls and post signs on your office door. One association executive was so bothered with constant phone calls that he left a voice mail message telling callers that he'd take return calls between 3 and 5 P.M. This was the time of day that he felt least able to concentrate on planning and oversight duties and most comfortable talking to people. Within three weeks, his powers of concentration and productivity rose dramatically. Callers readjusted their schedules to accommodate his.

Probably 90 percent of all your phone calls can wait for a few hours. As long as you have some time each day set aside for answering telephone calls, you'll be working at optimal efficiency.

Another advantage to answering telephone calls later is that you have time to arrange the information you may need for the call (see Figure 2-1 again). Have the appropriate folder on your desk when you return a call.

CHAINED TO A BEEPER

What if you have to wear a beeper or carry a cell phone as part of the job? If your employment is based on a contract, and this is increasingly true of top managers and executives, then you have some options for not being enslaved to your beeper. When it's time to renegotiate your contract, insert a clause allowing for specific times throughout the day or week when you expressly *are not* responsible for being on call.

If performance reviews and/or appraisals don't happen frequently enough for you where you work, or one is not slated until the distant future, arrange a meeting specifically to address this issue. After all, depending on how long you've been wearing the beeper, how many beeps you receive per day, the nature of your work, and how disruptive the overall effects have been, you don't want to let too many more days or weeks pass before elucidating your views. Surely there are stretches throughout the day and week where even your boss will agree that it's not mandatory for you to be wearing the beeper.

If most of your messages originate from a central source such as an executive assistant, instruct that person as to when it's okay for you to be contacted and when it's best to send messages later. You can use a system such as this:

FIGURE 2-2, REDIRECTING BEEPER MESSAGES

Level 1   Contact me now.

Level 2   Contact within X hours.

Level 3   Contact me sometime today.

Level 4   No need to contact me at all.

To make this system work, you decide in advance precisely what represents Level 1, so that Level 1 summoning of you is indeed rare. These would be absolute and dire emergencies where your input is absolutely essential.

PUT TRANSITION TIME TO WORK

Transition time, the five minutes it takes you to walk to your office or the 25 minutes to drive to work or the hour on the commuter train, can be used to increase your concentration. You can use this time, so often spent daydreaming or worrying, to focus your attention on the forthcoming meeting or task. If you foresee a tough meeting, don't fret. Simply contemplate the upcoming chore, put it into an overall perspective, and acknowledge its importance to your plan of action.

AVOID THE CLOCK; TIME YOURSELF

Use a timer rather than a watch or clock to keep track of time. The temptation to look at the time every five minutes is greater than most of us can resist. A timer with its face hidden, across the room or even tucked into a drawer, will alert you when it's time to move on to another task or to end your day.

RETURN WITH RENEWED FOCUS

If you absolutely can't bring your attention back to a task, try an overnight focus. Let it go for that day, but promise yourself to come to it with a new focus the next morning.

GIVE YOURSELF A CHALLENGE

If a task is boring, or you have difficulty concentrating, turn the task into a challenge. How many envelopes can you seal in ten minutes? How many different ways can you stuff a packet full of fifteen different pieces of information? Such techniques will make the time go much faster.

Creativity and Time Management

What does nurturing your creativity have to do with time management? Plenty! Creativity means taking novel approaches to problems and issues. People who follow the same routine daily could be wasting large chunks of time.

When you use creative approaches to the tasks at hand, it often leads to new time-saving breakthroughs and possibilities whether in your job or in your career marketing program. Here are some factors that can increase your creativity and save time.

CHECK THE WEATHER CHANNEL

Many people do some of their best creative thinking when the weather is overcast. The reasons for this aren't exactly clear. Perhaps a nice day filled with bright sunshine makes you want to be outside! Although you can't schedule a rainy day in advance, it does make sense to take advantage of what nature offers. If you're one of those people who think creatively when the weather outside is frightful, go with the flow. Review the long-term plan that's been sitting in your upper drawer for the past several weeks. Or arrange a brainstorming session with coworkers to overcome current problems.

ARE YOU A LARK OR AN OWL?

Studies confirm that most individuals do their best creative thinking early in the morning, although a significant number find their peak period to be midmorning or late at night. A minority are most creative in the evening. Finally, less than one in twelve are most creative during the afternoon.

If you're not sure what time of day you're at your creative best, monitor yourself over a one- or two-week period. Keep a time log of what activities you undertake and when—similar to checking your productivity cycle—and also note your energy level and enthusiasm throughout the various parts of each day.

In keeping this log, you may be surprised to find that you perform analysis, write reports, or undertake professional reading at a different schedule than you've been following.

NOTICE THE NUANCES

Other factors that may enhance your personal creativity include, but are not limited to, wearing comfortable clothes, clearing space on your desk, using your favorite writing instrument, or changing your posture (sitting, pacing, standing).

Also, you might try readjusting the height of your seat; experimenting with the type, size, and color or paper you use to write on; or even change the font and point size as well as background colors on your PC monitor.

WHAT'S HOLDING YOU BACK?

Factors that hinder concentration often hinder creativity, such as the ring of your phone, the color of your office walls, the presence or absence of background sounds, the sense of impending interruptions, or the feeling that simply sitting and thinking does not look productive.

Too little sleep or *too much* sleep won't help. Neither will skipping breakfast or consuming heavy breads and pastas for lunch. When your digestive system has lots of work to do, your brain is robbed of oxygen, which leads to the after lunch blahs! The solution is to eat a light lunch and take a walk afterward. I find that scheduling too tightly stifles my creativity; I can't think clearly when rushed.

DIVIDE AND CONQUER

Often you can break large, perplexing problems into smaller, more manageable issues. If a problem seems unsolvable, take a few minutes to think about it quietly. Make sure you will have no distractions, close your door, sit comfortably, close your eyes, and take several deep breaths. This advice is repeated so often that it seems like a cliche, but *it works!*

Once you break the big problem down, list the smaller tasks in priority order, and tackle them one at a time. Let's say you have a proposal to write for your company. Breaking it into eight sections will allow you to make a check mark next to each section as it is finished. That's eight mini-celebrations, rather than one for the whole proposal. Your feelings of accomplishment at the end of each small task will create more energy and confidence for you to move on to the next one.

Undoubtedly you've experienced days and weeks on end when you hardly had a moment to spare, let alone a moment to engage in highly creative thinking toward your career marketing efforts. Your ability to think creatively and strategically, however, is vital to your career.

A PROFESSIONAL IMAGE WORTHY OF YOU

What do they say when they see you coming?
—Steven Gower

ONE OF THE FIRST PEOPLE I ASKED FOR ADVICE when I decided to "go for it" as a sought-after author was a wardrobe consultant. Judy Turisi used to offer courses through a local adult education program on shaping your image through wardrobe. I hired her expressly for the purpose of coming to look at my closet.

On our first meeting, I opened up my closet doors. I was aware that several of my shirts were old, the collars frayed, and perhaps some of them didn't go with my coloring. Nevertheless, I was sure that at least one-half or so were salvageable. I thought I could round out my wardrobe by purchasing new ones as she recommended.

Less than thirty seconds after I opened the closet doors, she said in a clear, authoritative tone, "Throw them all out."

I was aghast! *"All* of them?" I asked.

Judy turned toward me and slowly and carefully said, "Read my lips—all of them."

For the balance of the afternoon, we discussed what I would need to buy, including what colors, what materials, and from which stores. Judy also looked at my ties (largely polyester) and told me to replace them all with silk. She looked at my shoes, she looked at my suits, she looked at my belts, and she looked at my overcoat. She even looked at my sock drawer.

From top to bottom, it was clear. What I wanted to project to others and what I was projecting were not in sync. It was futile to continue to wear what I was wearing because my clothes were simply functional. New York publishers, large conference meeting planners, and others whom I wanted to influence needed to feel "right" about me in their own ways. The only way to ensure that others would feel "right," at least from a wardrobe standpoint, was to dress impeccably.

After some moaning and groaning in the weeks that followed, I replaced my entire wardrobe, offering the remains to the Salvation Army and Goodwill Industries. Looking back, the whole process could have been simple, but oh, the things that get in our way before we finally make appropriate choices.

My goal of becoming a sought-after author and speaker was much more important to me than the lesser, never formulated or articulated goal of continuing to get as much use out of my clothing as humanly possible. So, my image had to change.

WHETHER WE LIKE IT OR NOT, IMAGE COUNTS

Image is not everything, contrary to Andre Agassi's oft-quoted line from a TV commercial. Image does speak volumes, however. Your overall appearance, facial expressions, age, gender, and body language compose a good part of the message you present to another person at your first meeting.

Think of your own first impressions of others. What do you usually notice first about a person? How does what you first notice affect the relationship? Would you listen more carefully to a man in a leisure outfit or to a man in a gray, three-piece business suit? Would a woman who couldn't meet your eyes make you feel comfortable about buying the product she is selling?

The problem with making a bad first impression or, worse, continually presenting a negative image is that the words you use won't matter. Effective communication, so vital to career advancement, simply won't occur. The other person won't be paying attention.

To advance your career, you need an image that enhances or complements the image that your company presents to clients. Does your firm present itself as dynamic, up-to-date, and vibrant? If so, your own image needs to reflect those qualities. In that case, you would probably wear brighter clothes and project a higher energy level than someone looking to advance in a conservative company priding itself on stability.

Knowing what image you present is more difficult than it would seem at first glance. Perceiving yourself exactly as others do is all but impossible. However, you can check your perceptions with those of a coworker or friend and combine that information with your own.

WHAT THEY SEE COUNTS FIRST

The statement, "I want to be promoted on the basis of my performance and not the way I present myself," typifies a common misconception of how the world works. People have little to go on when they first meet you *except* the way you look and act. Unfortunately, the first impression can be lasting, largely because people's perceptions are not easily changed, and because you may be likely to keep projecting the same image.

Your appearance and what that conveys are deemed part of your performance. Recognize that the way you look can affect the way you work and the way other people perceive your work. Cultivating your image means defining and focusing more sharply on who you truly are. Be authentic and genuine, and try not to mask aspects of who you are.

Your Image, Dissected

Appearance, facial expression, personal space, and body language all affect your personal image. So, give careful thought to all these factors (note the checklist in Figure 3-1 on pages 32-33).

APPEARANCE

Clothing, hairstyle, and accessories are important elements of how you appear to others. Dark colors are still preferred in professional clothing, especially for men. If you're a woman, and the powerful women in your organization always wear suits, take your cue from them and avoid wearing dresses or slacks. Keep your jewelry simple, preferably gold and never loud. Keep your fingernails manicured.

Even if red spiked heels are all the rage in Paris and New York, wear yours to social events, not to the office. Men need to pay close attention to wardrobe accessories such as shoes and ties. Understated clothes are generally safe in most office situations. During casual days, don't go too far by severely underdressing. Dress to blend in with the other professionals in your setting. Let your work stand out, not your fashions.

GRACE YOUR FACE

A broad, friendly smile puts across an image of trust that will serve you well. In addition to smiling, look the other person directly in the eyes, at a frequency that is comfortable for both of you.

Train yourself to become aware of how the facial expressions of others affect your own behavior. Does a coworker's smile that lasts a bit too long make you uncomfortable, or perhaps make him seem untrustworthy? Does a client's open smile allow you to feel comfortable around her? Once you heighten your awareness of this factor, among others we will discuss, you'll be better able to judge how your own mannerisms and appearance affect others—the first step to altering your image.

PERSONAL SPACE

How much space a person needs depends on the person and the situation. Standing close to someone generally means that you feel you have more power than the other person does. It usually makes people uncomfortable, so only do so when you need to assert yourself. Conversely, a person who continually backs away may seem afraid or untrustworthy.

Al, who was a minister before switching to sales, felt comfortable standing close to people. He did not stand close as a power play; it was the nature of his former profession. However, standing close to others is inappropriate in sales, and Al repeatedly had problems with prospects. So, judge the space with which another person feels comfortable rather than relying on your own comfortable distance.

Experiment with personal space to see where you feel most comfortable and how your distance from others makes them feel.

BODY LANGUAGE

Your posture and bearing tell others how you feel about yourself. And that tells your supervisors if you are able to advance. An erect, relaxed bearing promises confidence and competence. Watch out for nervous habits. You may not be aware that you drum your fingers on the desk or push back your fingernail cuticles. Such actions, however, are a dead giveaway to nervousness or a lack of confidence.

FACTORS YOU CAN'T CHANGE

Skin color, gender, and age are also important image factors. Although you can't change them, you can recognize their effect and plan around it. Janet Elsea, author of *First Impression, Best Impression*, observes that skin color still "remains the most dominant characteristic of physical appearance in this society."

If your color does not meet the "expectation" of the people you're working with, "initially, seek to counter stereotypes by paying extra attention to your appearance, facial expressions, eye contact, and other physical attributes," advises Elsea.

In time, the importance of skin color as a first impression factor should decrease. As more women advance in business, the importance of gender as an image factor should decrease as well.

If you're a Generation Xer, you may be seen as brash or aloof. An older person, however, may be perceived as too conservative and technologically disadvantaged. Younger workers might stress their past successes; older people could emphasize their fresh approaches to problem-solving. Counterbalance the possible negative images that your age may convey by accenting the positive ones.

YOUR GOLDEN VOICE

Your voice is a key factor in your image. Voice characteristics include speed, loudness, pitch, tone, and articulation.

Dr. Elsea recommends taping yourself, either in conversation or reading aloud, the first thing in the morning (when you're most relaxed and fresh), in the early afternoon (when stress and exhaustion tend to be high), and late evening (when you are relaxed but tired). By taping, you may discover one or more of these typical problems:

- Monotony, a lack of variation in pitch levels, may be interpreted as boredom or a lack of interest.
- A rising or upward inflection at the end of sentences give the impression of tentativeness.
- Talking through your nose is distracting to listeners (To find out if you are a nasal speaker, Elsea recommends pinching your nose closed and saying aloud, "Whoa, oh horse of mine." There should be no vibrations in your nose except for the word *mine*.) To correct this problem, open your mouth more and try speaking more loudly.

■ Stridency, or a shrill voice, conveys extreme nervousness. This is caused by insufficient breathing. Relaxation exercises, such as yawning, rolling your neck, and massaging your jaw, can help relieve this problem.

GET HELP WITH YOUR VOICE

Some voice problems require drastic correction. Katie was the vice president of marketing for a large architectural firm, but her high squeaky voice made her sound childish. Clients remarked that her voice did not fit her level of competence. She is currently taking speech lessons to lower her pitch.

If you pay attention to people who talk to you and notice who is most effective in speaking, the majority will tend to have a lower pitch and clear articulate manner of speaking. While the woods are heavily populated with people who slosh around when they converse, slur words, and mumble, effective speaking increasingly is becoming a highly demanded attribute of rising career professionals. There's no getting around it—nearly every organization wants technologically competent professionals who can reasonably articulate their thoughts.

PUTTING IT TOGETHER

The image factors covered in this chapter are only a subset of the countless factors that comprise the important career marketing tool known as "image." As an aid to analyzing your image, use the chart in Figure 3-1. It will also help you to decide how you can best change your image to your benefit.

If your image is not helping you to advance in your career, change it! This change is likely to take time, however, since long-developed behaviors are seldom easy to alter.

FIGURE 3-1, CHECKING YOUR IMAGE

Make three blank copies of this list. On one copy, describe the way you present yourself for each of the categories. For instance, under the category "shoes," you might describe your typical shoes as "black or brown, slightly worn heels with scuff marks on top." Or under the category "posture, bearing," you might describe your normal posture as "erect but not rigid." Then list what you think that conveys to other people. Using the "shoe" example, you may write that your typical shoes convey a careless attitude.

After you have filled out the form yourself, give one copy to a coworker you trust and the other copy to your spouse or a close friend. Ask them to write the same information about you. Use parts of each of the three perceptions to analyze your image.

Appearance	Description of my usual . . .	What that conveys . . .
Wardrobe:		
suit	_____	_____
shirts/blouses	_____	_____
ties/scarves	_____	_____
shoes	_____	_____
belts	_____	_____
coats	_____	_____
glasses	_____	_____
jewelry	_____	_____
briefcase	_____	_____
Personal Body Image:		
hairstyle	_____	_____
fingernails	_____	_____
beard or moustache	_____	_____
makeup	_____	_____
eyebrows	_____	_____
Physical characteristics:		
posture/bearing	_____	_____
facial expressions	_____	_____
nervous habits	_____	_____
hand gestures	_____	_____
eye contact	_____	_____

FIGURE 3-1, CONTINUED

Appearance	Description of my usual . . .	What that conveys . . .
Physical characteristics:		
personal space	_____	_____
touch	_____	_____
Voice characteristics:		
rate of speech	_____	_____
volume of speech	_____	_____
pitch (monotonous or singsong)	_____	_____
nasality	_____	_____
resonance	_____	_____
Atmospherics		
Automobile:		
year, make	_____	_____
exterior condition	_____	_____
interior condition	_____	_____
Office		
decor/pictures	_____	_____
desktop cleanliness	_____	_____
Accessories:		
type of pen	_____	_____
purse/wallet	_____	_____
business cards	_____	_____
cigarettes/cigars	_____	_____

CHAPTER 4

GET A CAREER COUNSELOR, COACH, OR MENTOR IN YOUR LIFE

When the student is ready, the teacher will appear.
—Zen Buddhist saying

YOU MAY HAVE NOTED that the title of Part I is "Steering Your Career," yet this chapter is about finding a career counselor, coach, or mentor. A contradiction? Nope.

Wherever you go, whatever you do in your career, you're the only one who will be there *every step of the way*. You will be making an endless number of decisions on your own. At any point along the journey, however, if you can get competent help, it pays to use it. Peers, parents, and mentors all may help. If you find a good career counselor, only a few hours a month will keep you focused on your goals and moving steadily toward them.

Does a Career Counselor or Coach Make Sense for You?

Before selecting a coach, you might want to ask yourself if such a person would be helpful. Psychologist Harry A. Olson, based outside of Baltimore, Maryland, observed that most professional and Olympic athletes have personal coaches to help them perform to their maximum potential and deal with competition.

The better such athletes become, and the more elite their status, the more they need and rely on coaches. Why? Because the higher they rise in their fields, the more critical their moves become, and the more vital personal feedback becomes in avoiding mistakes. A personal coach offers the competitive edge!

Like sports, business is highly competitive. In response to increased competition, many businesses are adapting and changing; some are being drastically overhauled. This breeds new insecurity and change. The career-conscious business professional needs to strategize more carefully and effectively than ever before to ensure success and to capitalize on new opportunities. Also, technology is advancing faster than our ability to comfortably keep pace with it. This has led to an increasingly rapid change in the quality and nature of personal demands on people's time and attention.

Enter the "career coach." Olson says that such a person can help "diagnose and sort out your situation and opportunities, offer new strategies for dealing with office politics and competition from other firms, and help you with vital stress-management skills. A good career coach helps you discover and capitalize on new opportunities, provides new tools to improve communication, and helps chart your goals and career path." Your career counselor is your personal, behind-the-scenes coach—a confidant, consultant, and resource.

DOING IT "MY WAY?"

"We don't question the wisdom of using tools to fix our cars or build wood projects, yet often we balk at using all the resources available to build our careers," says Olson.

Many achievers value "doing it on my own." They see using outside help as a weakness, as if they are dependent on the helper; as if using a personal consultant or counselor somehow takes something away from them. Far from it. The career counselor simply works behind the scenes, helping you so that you do your job better.

Earlier in my career, I used the career coaching services of Penny Yohay, then president of Taking Charge!, based in Alexandria, Virginia. We'd meet for only a short period each session, but I'd leave supercharged!

Self-analysis is limited and faulty because of self-protective "blind spots." A coach increases your objectivity. Also, because of his or her background and training, a coach can address a broader range of personal and career issues than you'd be inclined to do on your own. The coach's primary role is to be a trainer, a listener, an observer, a motivator, and a sounding board.

A good coach will help you discover your mission, assist you in mapping out your goals and strategies, and will monitor your progress. You will get objective, honest feedback on an adult-to-adult basis without moral judgments. The coach will neither command you to do something nor let you flounder. He or she will help you sort out options clearly and objectively. The ultimate decisions and actions are always your own.

Your goals and needs are always the specific foundation of your relationship with the coach. A good coach is committed to doing all that is in his or her power to help you meet those objectives.

Ultimately you alone decide if a coach or career counselor is for you. However, says Olson, if you encounter any of the following, you may benefit from what a coach could offer you:

1. Organizational changes within your company, especially if they have a direct impact on you.
2. Acquisitions or mergers.
3. Expansion into new markets.
4. Diversification into new products or services.

5. Increased competition to your company from other firms trying to take over your market share.
6. Increased management or supervisory responsibility.
7. Increased leadership opportunities.
8. A recent or soon-to-be-available promotion.
9. A new boss or leadership shake-up above you.
10. Changes in your role or assignments within your company.
11. In-company competition and power plays, corporate intrigue, jockeying for position, turf protection—especially if you're on the rise.
12. Blockades of your progress by internal feuds or informal political processes.
13. Excess stress on the job.
14. Increased media exposure or public speaking requirements.
15. Increased production or sales quotas.
16. A new project you lead or participate in developing.
17. Being a woman, an ethnic or racial minority, or being disabled.
18. Having a strong desire to advance in your company or field regardless of whether you experience any of the above.

CHOOSING MR./MS. RIGHT

If you're convinced that it makes sense to hire a coach, there are several steps to choosing the right one.

First, determine your needs. Once you've determined them, you can direct the coach as to how he or she can help you most. Your coach can also help you define your needs more explicitly.

The next step is to find the coach. The best way to begin is to seek referrals, use Internet search engines, or try the Yellow Pages under headings such as "Coaches," "Counselor," "Advisors," or "Consultants." Here is a brief roster of coaching-related associations:

FIGURE 4-1, COACHING ORGANIZATIONS

- Academy of Executive Coaching
  1304 Desoto Avenue
  Tampa, FL 33606
  813-258-1180

- Business Life Transitions
  2792 Main Way
  Los Alamitos, CA 90720
  310-598-8117

- Coach University
  2484 Bering Drive
  Houston, TX 77057
  800-48COACH

- Coaches Training Institute, The
  311 Richardson Drive, Suite B
  Mill Valley, CA 94941
  415-274-7551

- Hudson Institute of
  Santa Barbara
  3463 State Street, Suite 520
  Santa Barbara, CA 93105
  805-682-3883

- International Coach Federation
  2123 FM 1960 West, Suite 219
  Houston, TX 77090
  888-423-3131

- International Coaching Society
  4750 Vista Street
  San Diego, CA 92116
  619-282-5760

- Professional and Personal
  Coaches Association
  P.O. Box 2838
  San Francisco, CA 94126
  415-522-8789

- Professional Coaches and
  Mentors Association
  3020 Old Ranch Parkway,
  Suite 300
  Seal Beach, CA 90740
  714-220-9431

Olson recommends asking a lot of questions when you do identify some prospects. Most professionals today are used to being questioned by prospective clients.

1. Ask about training. What was his or her specialty?
2. Ask how their specialty relates to business if it isn't apparent.
3. Find out about experience related to coaching business executives. Also ask about experience working with high performance methods and motivation techniques. Has the person had any direct coaching experience in sports, drama, or speaking?

4. Check fee and payment arrangement. Some coaches will quote an hourly figure, some may work with you on a retainer basis.

5. If you feel that the person is probably not right for you, ask for a referral or two to other professionals so that you can check out other options before making a decision. Such a request will not offend a professional coach.

Serious, career-minded professionals are availing themselves of coaching opportunities more and more every day.

A Symbiotic Relationship: Mentor and Protégé

The word *mentor* traditionally brings to mind the picture of a gray-haired senior executive with wisdom and experience to share with the eager junior executive. Of the five mentors I have been fortunate enough to have, only one was a senior executive at an organization where I was employed. My other mentors were entrepreneurs operating their own firms.

One of my mentors was a man closer to my age with whom I had almost a "co-mentor" relationship. I also had a mentor I met only once—a luminary in the field of marketing with whom I communicated mainly by mail (this was before the widespread use of e-mail). It's also possible to have a mentor who does not give advice, but from whom you learn simply by example. Despite the possible varieties of mentor–protégé relationships, several denominators are common to all.

WHAT'S IT ALL ABOUT?

A mentor gives you *support* within the business world. If you're new to the business climate, it can seem full of rules and nuances that weren't taught in college. A mentor will guide you through the learning process, giving you clues to the subtleties of the workplace.

For instance, Bob takes his protégé, Zack, and a senior colleague, who is knowledgeable about company politics, out to lunch. Zack sits quietly, listening to the banter and picking up on skills, such as how to handle the check and how to be deferential or friendly to an executive of the company.

Knowledge and skills acquisition is another important part of the mentor–protégé relationship. It becomes an accelerated learning process for you. A mentor may read over your reports and give you feedback, take you to seminars, correspond with you via e-mail, or discuss your work with you regularly.

An associate tells of her mentor, Woody. "He was both a mentor and boss to me when I was just out of college. I wanted to be a writer but worked as a secretary. Woody set aside two hours every Wednesday afternoon to chat. He told me stories of his days at the *Buffalo Evening News*. We would talk about news events or the internal politics of our organization.

"The sessions were a formal way of reserving time for us when work, per se, didn't interfere," she says. Ten years later, their relationship was still strong. She'd send him clips of her articles, and he'd send her galleys of his books.

Yet, a mentor is usually not your boss. Having a mentor outside your organization or your division is maybe better in the long run. However, always be wary of a potential problem this may cause with your own boss, especially if he or she feels threatened by someone else giving you advice.

Broadened horizons are often available to you through your mentor. He or she will be pleased to introduce you to associates garnered over the years. When your mentor introduces you to key and interesting people, recognize that these are the types of individuals it may have taken you years to meet on your own.

The mentor–protégé relationship, however, is not a one-way street. The benefits to the mentor include:

- The personal satisfaction that comes with sharing knowledge and experience.

- The feeling that his or her work will live on.
- The ego boost to the mentor from imparting wanted knowledge (especially important as people age and ponder their usefulness).
- The excitement, added energy, and rejuvenation of spirit that come from sharing new ideas.
- The chance to reflect on his or her experiences.

The organization may also benefit by receiving training for its new or junior staff from experienced people.

This system has so many benefits that it has even been formalized. The U.S. Small Business Administration has a program called SCORE (Service Corps of Retired Executives). Retired business executives and people who are starting their own businesses set up meetings. The retired executives offer advice free of charge until the business owners no longer need or seek help. To find out more, visit their comprehensive website: http://www.score.org

NOT ALL IS ROSY

Problems can arise in the mentor–protégé relationship and there are some pitfalls to avoid. A common example is the junior who repeats the faults and weaknesses of the mentor. Emulating someone is helpful; blindly following someone is not.

Other possible drawbacks of the mentor–protégé relationship exist. These dangers are minor compared to the advantages; nevertheless, be aware of them in order to avoid them.

- The mentor may put in longer hours; mentoring takes time.
- A business or social failure by one person could embarrass the other.
- Each person risks getting involved in the other's career battles (in which neither belong) because of the bond that develops.

- Confidential information exchanged can leave one or both sides vulnerable if a rift occurs later.
- Rivals of the protégé who feel at a disadvantage might resent the relationship and seek to hamper the protégé's career.

Some protégés develop accelerated expectations. A mentor can make it look so easy; he or she simply calls someone on the phone and lands a big contract. Be comforted by the realization that it took your mentor a decade or more of experience and networking to be able to do that.

One survey revealed that only about a third of mentor–protégé relationships last more than three years. And in the cases in which the mentor was the immediate supervisor to the protégé, many times the protégé ended up getting fired!

Obviously these kinds of results call for a different approach to mentoring. "We've got to understand that mentoring is much more than just one relationship," states Kathy Kram, Ph.D. "It is a *system* of relationships that provide support."

WHERE TO FIND A MENTOR

The best approach to mentor–protégé relationships seems to be to seek as much help and advice available from as many qualified sources as possible. If you can establish a mutually satisfactory relationship with but one senior executive, that's certainly a start. However, don't isolate your efforts to finding only one mentor. Rather, widen your view of your environment and absorb as much information and experience as comes your way.

The ideal possible mentor is an executive retired from your organization and hence outside the mainstream of office politics, while still able to chronicle the events leading to the current political situation. A retired mentor will have more time, and therefore be more likely to do favors for you, and to actually teach you.

PART II

MARKETING ON THE JOB

CHAPTER 5

KNOWING WHAT MAKES YOUR ORGANIZATION TICK

*Intelligence is quickness in seeing things as
they are.*

—George Santayana

EVERY ORGANIZATION IS DIFFERENT, if not in the products or services it provides, then in other, more subtle ways. At XYZ Video Productions, the expected attitude is an aggressive, "go-grab-the-world" one. If you're at DEF Systems down the street, a quietly professional demeanor is vital for dealing with both company insiders and clients, who have come to expect such an attitude. And at RST Financial Services around the corner, conservatism and caution are the watchwords even if they mean missed opportunities for business.

Knowing what makes your organization tick is important in your career marketing efforts, at least for the short term. Realistically assessing your organization's policies and procedures (and the underlying rationale for having them) will enable you to know how best to get ahead in the prevailing environment.

On my first job, as a marketing representative for a *Fortune 500* computer manufacturer, I soon learned that the way to impress the boss the fastest was to:

(1) make the quota (obviously), and
(2) spend as little time in the office as possible.

The prevailing climate at our branch office was, "If you're in the office, you can't be out selling" (Never mind that the more you sold, the more you had to administer and report).

In other organizations, other unwritten rules prevail. In the federal government, unfortunately, the prevailing rule tends to be, "Don't show too much enthusiasm for your work." My fifteen years in the metro Washington, D.C., area convinced me that the federal government is structured to reward mediocrity (although such is not true in every agency or department).

Let's examine techniques you can use to accelerate your understanding of the organization for which you work.

ORIENTATIONS: SLAP-DASH OR COMPREHENSIVE

Most larger organizations have formal or informal orientation programs for new employees. Orientations can offer a wealth of information about your organization immediately. I've known of companies where orientation lasted one hour—long enough for the new employee to sign W-2 forms and hear about vacation and sick leave policies. A policy manual is shoved at the new people, who are then sent to their desks. Hence, employees learn about the organization by what is *not* said at orientation.

Other organizations go much further in their efforts to bring new employees on board. They spend days with a newcomer, getting that person up to speed on the organization's structure, philosophy, past experiences, and future goals. New hires are introduced to all the current employees. Some companies develop videotapes that show employees and clients in action or illustrate different areas of the company.

During your orientation, ask to see copies of the office memoranda distributed in the previous two or three months. Reading these will help you assess the current work flow and political atmosphere.

READ THE WALLS!

Your organization's walls and bulletin boards are a gold mine of information about its workings. Read the plaques on the lobby walls. If the plaques are awarded to company employees from outside organizations, they can tell you what other companies, agencies, or community groups are important to the image of your company. If the awards are from your organization to its own employees, they will tell you the characteristics and skills valued by the organization.

Bulletin boards filled with employee newsletters as well as suggestion boxes indicate organizations that consider the input of employees to be important. A bulletin board with notices and announcements from upper management, but no opportunity for employee input, tells a different story.

A simple decorating change can foretell a change in company directions. For instance, a company I worked with took down its wood panels and a wall full of awards, painted the lobby a bright pastel, and exhibited modern art—big paintings with slashes of color. It became apparent that this was the precursor of a change in target market from small family-owned businesses to international corporations.

The walls of individual offices in your company can be just as full of information. Check the pictures that your supervisor hangs on his or her walls. Are there patterns in the types of pictures used to decorate the offices of executives in your company as opposed to those of staff workers? Which type does your own office resemble?

WHILE YOU WAIT

Many skillful salespeople know the discoveries available in an organization's reception room. A good place to start is the magazines on the coffee tables or on the racks. The types of magazine displayed reveal something about the business. If an international travel magazine is on display, the firm most likely takes a global approach to business. If *Forbes, Fortune,* or similar publications are displayed, the business is projecting an image of sophistication and awareness of corporate life.

The receptionist can give an indication of your company's philosophy, too. Generally speaking, a more mature receptionist may reflect management's desire to maintain an image of a well-established, reputable, traditional business, whereas a younger person in fashionable dress suggests a company that is fast-paced, energetic, and "on the move."

The layout of the reception room itself is another clue. A company that shields its employees from view usually has a high regard for them and is trying to convey a high-class image.

IT'S IN THE BOOK

New employees often receive company policy manuals when they join a firm. And, almost without fail, no one reads the manuals. Although the reading may seem dry, be the first on your block to read through your policy manual and make notes about what you don't understand or where you see opportunity.

Beyond procedural matters such as regular office hours, time sheets and benefits, policy manuals will often discuss company goals, the responsibilities of different positions, and promotion policies—valuable information for moving ahead.

Acquire Company Expertise—Become an expert on the formal policies and goals of your organization. Collect all the materials published on its goals, policies, and statistics. Be the one person in your division or department that others can count on for answers.

VISIT THE WEBSITE

I'm still amazed by how often I encounter entire audiences either at annual conventions or at company meetings where hardly anyone in attendance is familiar with their own organization's website. Granted, many sites are geared for customer and other non-organization members. Still, there is so much information to be gleaned at your own organization's website, and so little effort to visit, that it makes perfect sense to visit, *today.* The same observation can be made regarding any intranets and other special online addresses where you can gain a great deal of information about your organization in a hurry!

LET'S DO LUNCH

Lunches are an important part of an organization's social activities. And social activities are vital to your career advancement. Your participation in social events will increase the number of people you know in the company and will serve as evidence of your ability to get along.

Use lunches as an opportunity to meet and get to know other people in your organization, especially those in divisions that complement yours or to which you might someday wish to transfer. At the beginning of your employment, I recommend finding a soft touch in the office, a person who knows everyone and everyone's business and who likes to talk. Take that person to lunch and listen. Find out the names of the hard touches, the people who may be harder to get to know. Then invite *those* people to lunch. You may be surprised at their gratitude.

COMMUNICATION AND NON-COMMUNICATION PATTERNS

We'll call him Eric Lamp. He's the founder and president of a small company that produces educational CD-Roms. He proclaims an open door policy, encouraging his staff to come see him "any time you want." Although Lamp professes an open door policy, he creates an atmosphere in company staff meetings indicating that he prefers to solve problems by himself, and that he considers outside help an interference.

When Gwen, a new employee, knocks on his door with a suggestion for a more efficient filing system, Lamp thanks her and quickly ushers her out of his office. She never hears one word about her suggestion and notices that nothing happens. Lamp figuratively slammed his open door in Gwen's face by not showing interest and not providing any feedback, good or bad.

Executives often rate communication among themselves as their principal area of difficulty—more problematic than handling conflicts, holding better meetings, or making decisions. If executives find it difficult to have probing, problem-solving conversations among themselves, imagine how much more difficult it is for them to communicate effectively with staff members throughout the organization. Chances are that they avoid it when possible.

Although formal methods of communication, such as publishing a company newsletter or giving all employees a copy of the mission statement, are important, often they can be superficial attempts that push honest communication to the background. True communication, the kind that helps maintain committed employees and probably helps the profit sheet as well, is the kind where workers feel they have a stake. Face-to-face meetings are the best, since they allow the most possibilities for dialogue.

OPEN OR CLOSED COMMUNICATION?

Ask yourself the following questions about communication in your organization to determine if your firm is open or closed.

- Am I encouraged to make suggestions to my supervisors?
- Do I get feedback when I make a suggestion? Immediate feedback as well as long-term feedback?
- Does the person show a genuine interest or seem to be pacifying me?
- Do I have a clear picture of where my company is heading and how I fit into the picture?

If your organization has a pattern of open communication, take advantage of every opportunity to learn of the latest developments, to make suggestions, and to provide input. If the pattern is closed, outwardly trying to obtain information or attempting to provide input may get you marked as a pest. So figure out how to get noticed without negative connotations. For instance, if direct communication is not possible, maybe the top officers get their information through reports. Who else is privy to such reports? Perhaps you could volunteer to write them. If so, make sure you're credited.

HIRING FROM WITHIN

A friend I'll call Barbara Post, who works for the Human Resources Division of a large telecommunications firm, said to me, "I haven't done any recruiting or outside advertising for positions in more than two years. Our whole division is geared to promoting people from within the company and finding slots for displaced workers."

Barbara's is not the only company that has decided it's better to promote people from inside the system rather than going outside for new help. Many companies advertise positions via company intranets and on bulletin boards months before the same jobs are advertised outside the company, if that is even necessary.

Even if you're comfortable with your current position, it's nice to know that you have opportunities to move both vertically and horizontally in your own firm, maintaining your medical and retirement plans while changing your job responsibilities.

Promotion from within serves your organization as well. It creates less need for retraining and hiring outsiders and provides beneficial continuity.

To discover whether your organization promotes from within, regardless of the formal policy, talk to the people at your level and above. How long have they been in the organization? Did they come up through the ranks? If most of the people you talk to came in as new blood at their current positions, you may want to start looking for a firm that promotes from within.

GREAT PRODUCTS AND SERVICES, GREAT COMPANY

It's hard to be happy in a job where you're part of a company that produces shoddy products or gives poor service. It may also hurt your career development if you don't plan to stay with the same company for a good stretch. A receptionist I know, who worked for an engineering firm in Virginia, left her job because of the daily telephone complaints.

Though she had nothing to do with manufacturing the product that the company sold and had a relatively high paying position, she quit. "I didn't want to be connected with a company that kept getting complaints," she said.

Evan McGrath, on the other hand, works as a file clerk for an architectural firm. He points out the buildings his firm has designed to all his friends and relatives and clearly is pleased to be with the company.

The value of your pride in your work is not merely economic. It is spiritual as well, the feeling that you have done the best you could from beginning to end. No matter how well you do your own job in a company, you cannot be proud of your contribution if the end product is of poor quality. Staying with a losing outfit does damage to career marketing.

Still, a stint with a less-than-top-notch company can be a valuable learning experience. You may even find that working for such a firm can provide you with worthwhile opportunities to handle many different and important tasks and assignments—since there may not be many other employees who are willing or able to do them well! In general, however, your career will best be served by associating yourself with the most respected companies in your industry.

SHARPEN YOUR SKILLS:
CORPORATE TRAINING PROGRAMS

Corporate training programs can be wonderful career marketing tools. Each time you attend a training session, you're increasing your overall market value. What you learn in those sessions may well support existing or future goals.

I worked for the Burroughs Corporation (now Unisys) for about a year—I had recently received my MBA and was frustrated that I wasn't using all the great tools that I had been taught. During the course of my year with Burroughs, I was sent to a two-week training school in Lexington, Massachusetts, focusing specifically on sales techniques. That two-week course, some two decades ago, proved to be quite valuable. I was a good student and faithfully followed the curriculum. The methods of prospecting, handling objectives, and closing on sales have become an ingrained part of my overall marketing capabilities and have served me well in every subsequent job and endeavor. In fact, I was able to fuse what I learned into two books.

If you're new to the job market or are considering changing employers, there are many excellent books available on corporate training programs. In any case, you can always approach your boss with the idea of influencing him or her to send you to training programs you've identified.

If those programs serve the needs of your corporation by increasing your capabilities, and serve your overall career marketing efforts, you've got a great reason to pursue them.

If you learn of a program that you feel you must attend and your organization won't pay for it, pay for it yourself. Over the course of my career, I independently enrolled in Evelyn Wood Speed Reading, the Dale Carnegie Course, the Creative Wellness Program, a convention on community development, an annual writers convention, and the National Speakers Association Convention, among numerous other events offering seminar workshop and training sessions. Every one of them was worth the investment.

There is nothing more incongruous than a potential rising star who is tight with a buck when it comes to investing in his or her career. You have blown a lot of money a lot of different ways, and spending it on training that will offer you a more favorable future is money well spent.

MAKING YOURSELF INDISPENSABLE

*The only way to find the limits of the possible
is by going beyond them to the impossible.*
—Arthur C. Clarke

A N EFFECTIVE MARKETER CREATES A NICHE for the product or service that he or she is promoting; so too, you need to create a niche for yourself to effectively advance your career. Creating a niche involves making yourself indispensable—becoming the kind of person supervisors ask for first when reorganizations begin, the office expert on a particular technical subject, or the mentor to many of the organization's junior employees. Finding out what's needed on the job (not just what is expected) and doing it will get you noticed quickly.

Keys to Becoming Indispensable

How do you become the kind of employee your organization can't live without? Believe it not, you don't have to be extraordinarily gifted to accomplish this. It simply requires following a few simple methods, such as:

- Taking the unwanted job.
- Going the extra mile.
- Working harder when unsupervised.
- Getting credit for your group.
- Making your boss look good.
- Handling key client development.
- Becoming a mentor.
- Being aware of a supervisor's needs.
- Knowing what's needed.

Later in this chapter, we focus on how you can move from being an *indispensable* employee to an eminently *promotable* employee.

TAKING THE UNWANTED JOB

Martin was new to the consulting firm, brought in as one of a well-established group of trainers and instructional designers. Rather than melting into the pot of professionals versed in education, Martin became an expert in a software spreadsheet program that greatly facilitated project planning.

All of the company's records were being changed over to this program. Oddly, most of the firm's professionals had no interest in learning about it.

Martin, however, saw a niche for himself. The president of the company needed someone who could explain the software program and its applications so that instructions could be given to others. Martin stayed after work at least twice a week to become an expert at the software. Soon, anyone with a question about it was referred to Martin. In short, Martin became indispensable.

Similarly, you can develop your own niche by picking up a skill or technical knowledge that is vital to your company, yet relatively hard to learn. Be the best at something that no one else wants to do, and you'll dramatically raise your level of importance to your organization.

GOING THE EXTRA MILE

To get ahead, periodically take on more work than you're assigned. Volunteer to help on a project that is running over deadline and make yourself available for extra projects. You'll be noticed.

Frequently, companies need assistance with rush jobs. At the consulting firms where I've been employed, I always volunteered to work on proposals. Because a quick turnaround is necessary, volunteers are greatly appreciated. Also, working on proposals exposed me to information outside of my department and to people I did not work with on a day-to-day basis.

Jill, a coworker, was called the "Jill of all trades," a name of which she was proud. When a project required short-term assistance to bring it to a close, Jill was asked to take on the extra work in addition to her own project. She was able to switch gears quickly from one project to another and had soon worked with everyone in the company at least once, a unique feat. Her broad experience led to her rapid promotion within the following two years. Although going the extra mile may not always pay off so quickly, the reward will eventually come.

Ellen was a new accountant at a mid-size firm. Austin was having family problems and his work had been poor over the previous few weeks. Ellen began to finish Austin's projects, often working until late in the evening. Without bringing attention to herself by complaining or by making it obvious that she was staying late, Ellen greatly helped a fellow worker. This was eventually acknowledged by management as well as her peers.

You can go the extra mile in other ways. Do the little things that make a difference to your project. For instance, I prepared client reports in a company three-ring binder. This was not usual procedure, but I took it upon myself to do this extra work. It made a great difference in the way the reports looked to clients—and to my boss.

WORKING HARDER WHEN UNSUPERVISED

The scene occurs in thousands of offices every day. The boss is away, on business or vacation. A great sigh of relief goes up the minute he or she is out the door. People drift into each other's offices, the telephones light up with personal phone calls, people log on to fun sites on the Internet, and lunch hours are stretched to the maximum.

Managers report productivity to be only two-thirds of normal when they're not in the office. That's why working, even at your normal pace, when they're away will impress your supervisors.

My strategy during this time, always, was to work extra hard. I knew the boss was likely to monitor employee performance following periods of his absence, rather than while being in the office for an uninterrupted stretch of days.

To add to your indispensability, when supervisors are away, strive to complete jobs they assigned before their departure. There is nothing a supervisor appreciates more after a trip than, "Here's the job you wanted. It's done." The subtle, yet deep-seated message you convey is long-lasting.

GETTING CREDIT FOR THE GROUP

Getting credit for the entire group of people you work with can advance your career. This seeming irony—standing out by praising the group—makes sense in an overall business context. Those who make it to the top levels of management are the people who are able to motivate others to do their best and to work well in group situations.

What are you actually saying when you say, "My team did a great job?" Those above you know that when a group does well, it's at least partly because someone exhibited leadership. Highlighting the team is especially useful when you are the group's manager. It indicates your ability to facilitate good work.

MAKING YOUR BOSS LOOK GOOD

Similar to the concept of getting credit for the group of people you work with or manage, making your boss look good can only reflect favorably on you. Both your boss and his or her supervisors will appreciate this.

The best way to make your boss look good is to handle your work efficiently and thoroughly. If your boss is fair, he or she will give you credit for the work, increasing your chances of promotion. If your boss is not doing his or her share of the work, leaning on you unfairly without giving you the credit, it's still likely that you'll be promoted when your boss is promoted. That person knows you've been doing more than your share, and he or she won't be able to take a new position without your help. Handling your boss in difficult situations is examined more fully in Chapter 8.

HANDLING KEY CLIENT DEVELOPMENT

If your job involves working with clients who do business with your organization, particularly key clients on whom your firm depends, you're already positioned to become indispensable. Each time you interact with the client, either by mail, online, or in person, you're planting the seeds of a personal and professional relationship.

If you've done your job well and have proven time and again that you are a professional upon whom the client can rely, your relationship with the client, in part, becomes one of your company's important assets. As such, your relationship needs to be protected much as other tangible assets, such as the plant and equipment, are protected.

An important caveat to developing key client relationships is to avoid threatening your supervisors, professionally speaking, by undermining, overstepping, or otherwise harming the relationships they may have with clients.

Wherever you work, bringing new business into your organization will surely vault you to the head of the class. Whether you have direct marketing responsibility or not, be prepared. Developing new clients is time-consuming and rigorous. However, when you do land a client, surely you'll be the one they trust, the one they've known from the beginning.

BECOMING A MENTOR

Maybe you're only twenty-seven years old, or maybe you've only been with your present firm for a year and a half. Yet, with your previous experience and achievements, you may already be in a position to serve as a mentor to junior members of your organization. This can be accomplished on an informal, ad hoc basis, and you can literally choose the amount of energy you're willing to commit. Helping junior members always looks good to those above you, especially at performance review time.

I always gladly accepted the role of ad hoc mentor to junior associates by distributing reprints of material that I knew was directly helpful in accomplishing their present tasks. At one consulting firm where I was a project manager, I produced a fifteen-page information resource booklet that I distributed to everyone in the company. This booklet was a compilation of names, phone numbers, and addresses of frequently called libraries, government agencies, and other information services. It was of great use, particularly to junior staff who were not familiar with some of the entities listed. Now, instantly, they had a complete resource file at their fingertips.

BEING AWARE OF A SUPERVISOR'S NEEDS

Receiving praise is a primary human need. Yet, how often do we remember to praise our bosses? They are people, too. If your boss has been extra supportive of you, tell him or her that you appreciate it. Remember to praise your boss to your coworkers and other supervisors.

Be honest. A phony attempt can be detected immediately. Still, everyone has some good points that can be praised.

Be aware of any special quirks your supervisor may have. If he or she is feeling personally insecure about a particular client or project, help out and give the credit to your boss instead of taking it for yourself. You may need similar support some time in the future.

KNOWING WHAT'S NEEDED

One way to become truly indispensable is to be on top of your job, your department's goals, and your company's objectives. This three-way strategy includes reviewing your job description, deciding precisely what your department's goals are, and determining your company's objectives. Let's take a brief look at each.

First, knowing your job description and honoring it, or amending it if necessary, will protect you from any misunderstandings. It will also give you an idea of the part you play in the total picture of the organization, an important factor in your work satisfaction and chance of promotion.

Your job description ideally contains *all* the important activities of your position, the knowledge you need to have or acquire to perform those activities, and some sense of your overall role.

If your job description does not adequately detail the information you need to know and the responsibilities you have, now is the time to change it.

Second, learn and understand the goals of your part of the company. By whatever method your organization is broken into groups—department, division, project team—your group has objectives. As discussed previously, goals are important to guide actions as well as to mark milestones. Knowing your group's goals will help you to set priorities for your own work and make wise decisions concerning how jobs can best be done.

Finally, be aware of your organization's mission. Any organization, from the smallest business to the multibillion-dollar corporation, has a mission. If you don't already know it, find out. Your organization's brochure, annual report, promotional literature, or employee handbook will have the mission spelled out. The mission will unify and give meaning to all the division or department goals. Although conflicts among divisions will occur because of the nature of different responsibilities, a solid base can be produced when all employees realize the overall mission of the organization.

If you're unsure of the direction to take on a particular project and are not receiving sufficient guidance, look at the problem in light of your company's mission. Is what you're doing in line with a mission? Will it be good for the company in the long run? Your ability to make the correct decisions will be greatly enhanced by your awareness of your job description, your group objectives, and the organization's mission.

Keys to Promotion

Suppose you follow the guidelines discussed in the first part of this chapter and become indispensable. Are you guaranteed a promotion? Not necessarily. Conversely, making a big mistake in your job probably won't keep you out of the running either. The career track of those who get ahead hardly ever shows an uninterrupted rising trend line. It's a zigzag—uneven, going this way and that, but eventually to the top. However, there are some key ways to increase those upward "zags" and turn your job experiences into promotions.

ANTICIPATING ORGANIZATIONAL CHANGES

The usual promotion occurs because someone has resigned or has moved on to another position in the organization. In addition to filling such a vacancy, you can create your own promotion by being aware of organizational changes before others are and carving out your own niche in the new structure. As your organization expands or shifts its focus, be on the lookout for needs that you can fill on the new organization's chart.

Consider Caryn, formerly an assistant editor of a hobby magazine. Although she had advanced quickly, her chances for further growth were not good since her supervisor was well entrenched in his position. Recognizing that she needed a chance to grow, Caryn began calling her network of publishing friends and making efforts to get a job with another magazine. Then, from some remarks her publisher made at a farewell luncheon for one of the secretaries, Caryn learned that a plan was in the works to buy another hobby magazine about doll collecting.

She acted quickly and went to several area doll shows, getting ideas from the exhibitors on what they wanted in a magazine. When the publisher announced a special staff meeting, Caryn went to him that day with strategic plans for the new magazine and a table of contents for the first issue. When he reported the acquisition at the staff meeting, he also announced Caryn as the new editor. She saw an opportunity and took aggressive, appropriate action to make the best of the chance.

BECOMING AN EXPERT

Individuals who become indispensable in some aspect of their organization may get promoted, even if a new title has to be created for the position. Alec became his company's expert on HTML, someone who could answer any question on the topic. His office extension became the hotline for quick information. Because he took over a function that the company hadn't required before, it took some lobbying on his part, but he was named Director of Web Development. It was a new position in the company and a nice promotion for him.

In your present organization, are you developing expertise on a particular topic? If so, make your superiors aware of your special knowledge and the extent to which people depend on *you* to provide that knowledge. Or, if there is an area in which you feel that your department is sorely lacking—perhaps, market research, coordinating function, or follow-up work— choose to be the one to fill the gap. Chances are you'll reap the rewards of career advancement.

TAKING CHARGE OF YOUR
PERFORMANCE REVIEWS

In my years as a management consultant, I came to the conclusion that performance reviews were all too often unfair
and sometimes counterproductive. Most managers see them
as a necessary evil and give their employees only a perfunc-
tory review. Yet despite the prevailing problems inherent in
the performance review system, this is *still* the one time
during the year, quarter, or review period when you and
your boss can sit down specifically to discuss *you*. I've found
that it's often possible to turn these matter-of-fact sessions
into opportunities for promotion with a little career marketing "homework."

The key is to keep vigilant track of your own performance
throughout the year. I used to evaluate myself quarterly,
without fail. All you need to do is review your appointment
book and your list of goals and other planning aids and com-
pare how you've done versus what you set out to do. Then,
write up your own mini-evaluation using lists and descriptive
sentences. Three areas to cover are objectives, skills, and
inventory, the latter being simply an overall description of
your performance during the last three months.

Armed with your own self-appraisal, you can take more
control during the performance review session with your
boss. By being able to point quickly to concrete accomplishments, you might avoid simply being labeled with a numerical
performance rating, slapped on the back, and sent on your
way. More likely, your boss will remember what you've said
and will take your case to those higher up in power. An additional perk of the self-appraisal system—no matter what the
outcome of your performance review—is that it keeps you on
your toes in your career-marketing efforts and may even help
you to sell your skills and experience to another company.

PREPARING YOUR BOSS

Your boss is vitally important to your career advancement and, as such, needs to be prepared for such an eventuality. A supervisor who is confident of his or her own abilities and chances for success will be pleased to see you move up. In this case, share your advancement ideas with your supervisor. Let that person know that you seek and will work for more responsibility and more independence, and that it will look good for both of you to the rest of the company.

Take care, however, with a manager who's afraid that you're after his or her position. People who feel threatened have a tendency to protect themselves. Your forward progress could be delayed by your manager's fear. With such a manager, it's a good idea to indicate that your advancement will be a boon rather than a threat. Failing that, you may have to make allies of your supervisor's supervisors and other influential people in your organization.

Also consider the needs and desires of your supervisor. Is he or she content with the current position or also looking for advancement? Knowing that will allow you to analyze your chances of taking over his or her job and will give you an idea of the rewards and negative features that such a promotion would entail.

A promotion, per se, does not automatically mean you're advancing along your chosen career path. You can also be promoted to what proves to be a dead-end position or to one that diverges from the path you are seeking.

In evaluating the worth of a promotion, consider two different factors—the overall strength and stability of the company, and the visibility and opportunities of the position to which you're being promoted. Look ahead several positions in the ladder above your current position. If you're an account executive and want to be regional director of marketing, carefully watch the person in that position now to determine how to respond to situations. "Living ahead" will keep your eyes focused on the correct path and stretch your brain to thinking through the types of situations you yourself will face one day.

CHAPTER 7

OFFICE POLITICS AND MARKETING YOURSELF

Always bear in mind that your own resolution to succeed is more important than any other one thing.

—Abraham Lincoln

Have you noticed? Office organization charts always look so nice and neat. Jason reports to Margaret who reports to David who reports to Damon . . . the lines are straight and direct. That's the *formal* power structure of the organization. It's important because it shows who has authorized power and is presented to the outside world as the official chain of command.

Charting the *informal* power structure in your office is a different matter. Knowing it is more important to your career advancement, however, than having a copy of the formal organization chart. The examples in this chapter will give you an idea of the elements that make up the informal power structure in your office.

The Informal Power Network

To fathom the informal power network, first make a list of the people in your division or department who normally have lunch together. Next to each group, note how long they've been socializing together. Then make notes on how the members of the group can impact your career. Your list might look like this:

FIGURE 7-1, INFORMAL POWER NETWORKS

Group Members	Time Together	Position/Effect
1. Kim, Adam, David, Kristen	3 months	Project managers; could broaden my horizons, allow exposure to different projects
2. Samantha, Julia, Loretta	8 months	Administrative; could help me learn more about company operations

The longer such groups have been together, the harder it can be to make inroads. However, these are the groups likely to have important information, and depending on how you strike them, they may embrace you as an insider.

Take note of any small groups that meet behind closed doors but are not working on an office project. A shift could be in the works. Whether it succeeds or not, stay tuned.

Notice who walks into the office of the department or division manager without an appointment. No matter where they're listed on the formal organization chart, these people have power.

The informal system is based on relationships among the people in the office. Its foundation is the grapevine—an information system as complete as the telephone company's—because knowledge is power. Power—your ability to make things happen, to control events—is the currency of career advancement. For example, Jeannette learned that her boss was planning to give an assignment that she wanted to her coworker, Ted. Jeannette was disappointed, but she prepared for it rather than hearing the news from her boss and reacting on a gut level to a decision already made. Acting on her knowledge, Jeannette approached her boss with several reasons why she wanted the assignment, without mentioning Ted at all. She got the assignment.

Be alert to office rumors that can expose you to opportunities, crises, and power shifts in sufficient time to plan your responses.

A mentor also can help you understand the power nuances within your organization or your profession. As already discussed, mentors enjoy passing on information, and those years of experience can be highly beneficial to you!

TO SUCCEED IS TO CREATE ADVERSARIES

If you're good at what you do, you're going to have adversaries. Using that unfortunate fact to your advantage is a good indication of your ability to play office politics. Determine your adversary's point of view so that your own will become more enlightened. Is your adversary more conservative about projected costs and time lines when writing proposals? Does he or she have different types of relationships with clients?

Analyze an adversary's tactics and use whatever might work for you. How does Marsha interact with the boss? What does Jeff say to the administrative staff so that his requests get handled quickly? Assess the motives of your adversaries and you'll understand your own motives better. Do they seek the position that you are seeking?

Listen to your adversary's attacks on you when and if they arise. Forget any personal feelings engendered by such an attack and listen for the important data that will surface from vituperative remarks—information about how you're perceived by others.

DINE OUT

Don't isolate yourself by eating lunch at your desk every day. Lunch conversations can give you valuable insight on peoples' attitudes toward the organization, their jobs, and each other. It's better to be on the edge of several different cliques than to get tied up with the same group every day for lunch. Invite someone to lunch from a different division in the organization. Use that time as an opportunity to find out what that division does as well as the chance to discover if you have similar professional interests.

"Do lunch" particularly if you are having problems with a coworker. The chance to discuss work issues in a different environment, or even to ignore work issues and try a social exchange, may be all that's needed to smooth the way for the work relationship.

Don't wait to be invited for lunch—you could wait forever. Act rather than react. If someone leaves your office saying, "We must have lunch sometime," take advantage of the opening. Call within a few days and suggest two or three times that you're free. People are more likely to accept an invitation when offered a variety of specific times.

Although it's more common for those higher on the power ladder to initiate lunch suggestions, don't be afraid to invite an executive above your level. Surprise moves can sometimes be effective attention getters. Many higher-ups may genuinely appreciate your initiative and professional aggressiveness.

Drinks and dinner after work play different roles depending on your organization. At one office where I worked, employees met for happy hour every other Friday after work. It was good as a morale builder. People whose work didn't bring them in contact with one another through the week would talk and joke during the Friday sessions.

Going out for drinks after work "with the gang" can be a friendly way to show team spirit and solidarity, particularly after a long, involved project. Have a beer, but if the rest of the crowd gets rowdy, stay cool. It's a lot easier to accept an apology from someone who had too much to drink the night before than to have to make apologies for your own behavior.

BODY LANGUAGE SAYS A LOT

Body language can be a rich source of information about relationships in the office. People who lounge in an office door may be demonstrating a lack of confidence about entering the room, or may be indicating to the person inside that they don't have the time to sit down. People standing or walking close to each other are probably allies; people who act friendly but look away while talking to each other are showing their discomfort or distraction.

Body language can also be a clue that a person is lying. A study conducted years ago by Dr. Robert Goldstein of New York University found that Americans tell an average of 1,000 lies per year. My guess is that that figure has increased greatly. Liars tend to:

- Have a brief, minimal change in facial expression
- Cut back on gestures and eye contact
- Lean forward less, shift in their seats
- Become self-conscious
- Adjust their clothing
- Scratch (!)
- Talk slowly
- Speak in shorter sentences than normal, thinking that the longer they talk, the more likely they are to give themselves away (They're right, they will give themselves away).

In some places in Southeast Asia it is believed that someone telling a falsehood blinks more rapidly than is normal for them.

Certain people—calmer types and men more than women—smile *more* when they lie, presumably because this is a gesture they can control. Other signs, such as a perspiring brow or flushed cheeks, may indicate that someone is uncomfortable rather than lying.

LEARN WHAT TOPICS ARE *IN* AND *OUT*

Every organization seems to have certain areas of discussion or topics that are off limits. So, depending on where you work, it may be necessary to stick with safe talk. What *is* safe talk? Where my brother works, for instance, all public conversations are trivial and focus on sports, weather, or company programs.

Getting into a hot political discussion in the elevator, however amicable and cogent, may stall or sink your advancement plans.

Review any public relations releases about your superiors. If, for example, civic organizations or volunteer work are prominently mentioned, you know that these activities are valued.

Learn enough about the organization rules to know when it's important for your career to blend in, and when it's important to stand out. Know where the crowd is going and why they're going there, without losing your individuality. Most of all, remember that politics is never a substitute for doing a good job.

Getting Along with the Production Staff

Other than the self-fulfillment that comes from treating each person with respect, there are several practical reasons for treating your organization's clerical and production staff well. The first is that good treatment tends to get your work done faster (and better) than the work of a person in the office who doesn't treat the production staff well. Production staff members may not be unprofessional enough to sabotage your work or do it poorly, since that would damage their own reputation as well as the entire organization's. Nevertheless, take note of the patterns in your own office.

If the assistant responsible for copying documents feels comfortable enough with you to ask questions, rather than directing such questions to his or her supervisor who must then relay them to you, the work will get done faster. And, obviously, the supervisor won't be bothered by a lot of questions that you can answer.

Another reason for having the production staff as allies is that they're a rich source of information. They know who turns in work on time and how complete it is, sometimes more accurately than the person's direct supervisor.

The owner of a mid-size architectural firm says that he learns more by taking the administrative staff out to lunch than from weekly progress meetings with his top managers. "They know who's making telephone calls about new jobs, who's slacking off work, who's coming in late, and who makes jokes about me and the other partners," he says.

Members of the administrative staff also talk to each other in the office. One insecure executive (and there is at least one in every firm) played tyrant to the production pool, asserting power that he wanted, but didn't have. Soon everyone in the office was aware of his unnecessary rantings and ravings to the production workers. His reputation quickly went down the toilet, and he eventually left for another organization.

Conversely, when a member of the production staff is asked for an opinion on how he or she is treated, good deeds will surely be appreciated and mentioned. The manager of the accounting department e-mailed the head of the production department of her company, praising her and the staff for their fast turnaround and accurate work on important financial reports.

The accounting manager cc'd a copy of the e-mail to the president of her company. The president was so pleased that someone had made the effort to notice the work of the production department that she took the accounting manager to lunch. The manager said that, although she hadn't planned the political perks that came from acknowledging the production staff, she certainly enjoyed them.

EASING THE PRODUCTION LOAD

Accurately estimating the amount of time needed for your project will win you big points with your production staff. If everyone in your office accurately estimates the time needed for their portions of projects, missed deadlines will be avoided, managers will have more time, and support staff will feel less stressed.

Respect the production scheduling process and work with the staff to adjust it only for emergencies. Working effectively with support staff can only make their lives simpler, and your life and career advancement smoother.

IS YOUR BOSS A ROADBLOCK?

Before following the leader, find out who the leader is.

—Dave Weinbaum

MANY BOOKS ARE AVAILABLE THAT OFFER managers advice on how to handle troubled employees. Often, however, employees find themselves working for managers whose actions, procedures, and styles may reduce productivity, create resentment, or demotivate subordinates. This chapter outlines the ways your supervisor may hinder your career advancement, as well as steps you can take to minimize the effects of this behavior.

Identifying the Problem

Do you suspect that you're working for a problem boss? For the sake of your own career, be on the lookout for certain types of attitudes and behavior in your immediate supervisor.

WORKER EXPLOITATION

An employee of a computer software firm in New England noticed that he was always being assigned to clients located at least three hours of driving time from the office. Although he recognized that on-site work was necessary, other employees in the firm with the same seniority were assigned clients who were within one hour of driving time. For a month, the employee kept a detailed log of the hours he spent driving to visit his clients. He also asked two of his friends in the same division to keep similar logs of their visits. At the end of the month, he requested a meeting with his supervisor and illustrated the differences in assignments.

In this case, the supervisor honestly had not realized that he was making assignments in such a manner, and he thanked the employee for bringing it to his attention.

Your supervisor, however, may not be so kind. If you approach your boss about feeling exploited, have a good paper trail to support your claims. Choose your words so as to allow the supervisor the option of admitting to an oversight. Critique his or her actions, not the supervisor's personality. "It seems I've been assigned a disproportionate share of the overtime work lately; in fact, 20 percent more than any of the other employees in this division. I wondered if you had noticed this?" That approach will undoubtedly work better than if you said, "You're sticking me with all the overtime and I'm tired of it."

READ THE FINE PRINT

A frequent trap that supervisors fall into is offering a manipulative promise to employees—the hint or outright declaration that a more favorable future is in store if someone accomplishes a desired goal. There's nothing wrong with making promises dependent on behavior or actions, but some managers don't hold up their end once you've done your part.

If you find yourself on the receiving end of promises that are re-evaluated every time a goal is reached, you might want to write a memo after you've received a promise. It could read, "My understanding of our discussion this morning is that I'll be given a promotion when my sales increase 20 percent over their current rate."

This spells out the promise and the action you need to take. Give the memo to your supervisor—and keep a copy for use as a gentle reminder if needed. Yes, a hard copy is preferable to an e-mail.

Closely related to the continuing promise is the dangling carrot. Does your employer ask more of you before you're due for a raise or a vacation? This form of coercion can, understandably, create resentment. I had a boss in Connecticut who used to increase my assignments for weeks on end prior to my being due for a raise.

Recognize such behavior, but don't fall into the trap of giving more than you've got. A good manager will seek to maintain an even keel and a balanced workload for you throughout the year. Resist the opportunity to let the supervisor back you into a corner before annual review time. Continue your work at a reasonable level.

PLAYING FAVORITES

If deferential treatment is the problem, this is one case where you may not be able to work with your supervisor, and may be forced to go above his or her head. If you're the individual being treated unfairly, first attempt to point it out to your boss in a constructive manner. An employee of a small advertising agency felt that she was always given the problem tasks, assigned to finishing projects that senior associates had fouled up. She openly explained her feelings about it to her boss. He replied that he considered her extremely useful to the firm. Her comments, however, made him realize that he hadn't given her adequate feedback, and he understood her feelings of resentment.

Putting your comments in the light of how the supervisor's behavior makes you feel will often take the heat off the manager, allowing him or her to focus on the behavior itself rather than taking the complaints personally.

If you notice that one or more fellow employees are being treated unfairly, point this out to your supervisor. You can bring this up by saying, "I notice that Sam and Ellen seem to feel that you treat them differently from the rest of us. I know you don't mean to do this, but I wonder if you'd noticed?"

Although there's a fine line between intrusive and helpful behavior, closing your eyes to the unfair treatment of fellow employees can backfire on you. You may one day fall out of your supervisor's favor and end up on the receiving end of the same type of treatment. It will be better for you and your organization if all employees are treated consistently.

EMPOWERED FOR FAILURE?

This practice is particularly damaging, not only to employees, but also to the overall company productivity and reputation. Supervisors "program for failure" when they give assignments that can't be completed successfully, or when they don't provide enough guidance or resources to finish the task.

To avoid programming for failure, know your own work schedule. How much can you accomplish in a given amount of time? What resources do you need to complete a certain job?

If you're given an assignment with a built-in time bomb, indicate this immediately. Don't wait until a day before the project is due before letting your supervisor know that it was impossible from the start. Also, once you realize a current project is in trouble, write down all the facts and make as close an estimate as possible of the resources and time necessary to save the project.

An associate of mine who was frequently caught in this trap designed her own weekly progress report with the aid of project management software. This allowed her to chart the time and resources used for each task, letting her supervisor know the problems in advance as well as providing a good baseline for estimating future projects.

BREAKING AND BENDING

Does your supervisor sometimes change the meaning of something that was said previously? Poor supervisors can get in the habit of "bending" what was assigned or said to suit their own current needs. It's obviously impractical to carry a tape recorder at work to catch every word your supervisor says. Still, you can ask for a further explanation of assignments or statements. Ask for a repeat of the assignment a day or two after you first received it. Your supervisor may have altered the assignment in his or her mind without telling you.

The flip side of the inconsistent manager is the one who's overly rigid when issuing assignments or maintaining work schedules. In the changing workplace of today, many employees have needs for flexibility in both the hours that they work and when assignments are due.

If you have a good reason for wanting to change a supervisor's order, first consider the benefits to you and the company (or client) before asking for such a change. Showing that increased productivity will usually get your supervisor's admiration for your logical thoughts, rather than resentment for trying to change orders without a reason.

NO FEEDBACK

Unfortunately, it seems that some supervisors have trouble giving feedback on positive developments, and no trouble offering feedback on problems! A lawyer friend once told me that his firm had not given him a raise in two years because of financial problems. He was unhappy about not getting the raise, but he was even unhappier about not getting any feedback about his performance. "I would've gladly stayed with the firm if they had given me regular performance reviews and explained how I was contributing to the firm. I could live without the extra money if I knew how I fit into the company's future," he said.

Feedback, both positive and negative, is vital to your performance and fosters an atmosphere of trust and cooperation. Most supervisors who don't give feedback aren't intentionally creating problems. Some people aren't in the habit of commenting on performance and don't understand its importance.

In that case, ask for it! As you hand your supervisor a report, say, "I'd like to hear your thoughts on this." If none are forthcoming, in time ask again. It may take awhile to "retrain" your employer to give you feedback.

A frustrating trait some mangers have is answering questions for feedback with one word, such as *fine*. Tactfully convey that you value your supervisor's experience and would appreciate specific positive or negative comments that could improve your performance.

Giving your supervisor appropriate feedback is another way to condition your supervisor to give *you* feedback. How many of us compliment our bosses on work well done? It's easy to forget that mangers need feedback, too!

Making the Problem Work for You

Your boss might be a terrible taskmaster, a tyrant of the office, insensitive to individual needs, or merely callous. He or she may be routinely morose, unsupportive, or guilty of exploiting workers. The list of potential management sins goes on and on. However, most of the people who complain daily about their bosses don't realize that there are actually some benefits to working for a boss that they don't respect. And there are ways to turn a bleak situation to your advantage.

Following are many things you can do to change the problems associated with having a poor boss into a boost for your career.

WORK ON YOUR PEOPLE SKILLS

Working for a boss whom you don't respect may strengthen your ability to deal with people—including good and bad future bosses—and it may help you hone your diplomatic skills as well. If you can peacefully coexist with people whom you don't respect, your chances of successfully dealing with all others will improve. This is an important side benefit for career marketers. In fact, one of the single most important traits for making it to the top is the ability to get along with others.

ASSUME A MORE ACTIVE ROLE

When your supervisor is an incompetent boss who lacks creativity and has trouble making decisions, turn the situation to your advantage by taking on more responsibility. Do some of your supervisor's work by thinking up solutions to problems and new programs or products. Be careful, however. If you do this, be sure to share your ideas with your boss first instead of taking them to colleagues or to your boss's boss!

THE BIG PICTURE

Perhaps you're working for an insensitive boss who, intentionally or otherwise, bawls you out for minor mistakes or takes credit for your achievements while neglecting to praise your efforts. It might seem like nothing positive can come from this experience, but don't despair. You're learning one of the most valuable of business lessons—"don't take it personally." Nothing stops a career dead in its tracks more than the tendency to take every callous remark or each instance of a lack of recognition as a personal affront. Successful career marketers don't dwell on these things; they move on.

STAY COOL AND CALM

Having a pressure cooker for a boss can be a nightmare and is certainly the cause of many an ulcer. However, rest assured that you're not the only one who notices your manager's volatile behavior. One strategy, then, in the face of his or her explosions, is striving to be a model of calm level-headedness. Your ability to stay cool and perform well, contrasted with your boss's temper tantrums, may eventually win you kudos from colleagues and from top management.

THE ADVANTAGE OF A BAD EXAMPLE

You can learn as much from a negative example as from a positive one. A friend of mine in the publishing business is constantly praised by his subordinates for his management style. When asked to what he credits these glowing reports, he told me that he kept meticulous mental notes of what his previous boss had done wrong, and he vowed to do the opposite when he was in a position of authority. So instead of wasting mental energy grousing about the things your boss is doing wrong, contemplate how they could be done right in the future.

IF YOU HAVE TO MOVE ON . . .

Sometimes, a bad boss can make your life so unpleasant and unrewarding that simply can have to escape the situation. Once you've determined that you can simply no longer stay in your present position (beyond the short run), you may find some comfort in knowing that you're leaving. If, for any reason, you've ever debated for months about leaving a position and you now find yourself confronted with a boss for whom you know you can't work, you'll probably regard this situation as beneficial.

All your mental anguish can subside, because as soon as the right position develops, you're going and you know it. There's light at the end of the tunnel. The daily drudgery and personal contact that you have eagerly sought to minimize are now, at least, palatable. The strains and pressures that may have followed you home can now diminish.

Once you have made the decision to go, however, keep your energies focused on procuring the next position. Don't dwell on why you're going or how good it will be when you're gone. The chances are fair that you will gain a new boss whom you can respect, but remember that there is also a chance that things could be worse.

HOLD YOUR HEAD UP

As long as you remain in your present position, keep doing a good job and uphold the name of your organization. To do anything else would be a strong reason not to respect yourself. Be professional and take your experiences in stride. Learn and benefit from them, but don't waste energy resurrecting the past.

Don't try to "even up" the score or fulfill your personal sense of justice. This is a waste of time, regardless of any minor psychic satisfaction. The long-term personal benefit to career marketing in gaining "revenge" is nil. Moreover, the possibility of something going wrong or being misinterpreted is high. When you need to leave, do it with dignity and class. That attitude will pay off in the long run.

PART III

THE IMPORTANCE OF INTERPERSONAL SKILLS

LISTEN WELL, MARKET YOURSELF WELL

The world is divided into two types of people: those who like to talk, and those who don't like to listen.

—James Thorpe

ALTHOUGH WE LEARN HOW TO READ, SPEAK, AND write as children and are encouraged to hone these skills throughout our lives, we rarely, if ever, receive any formal training in listening or pay attention to its importance in our lives.

People spend nearly half of their communication time listening. Good listening is an active, complex process that takes knowledge of a few basic tenets and lots of practice. In a professional or personal relationship, it pays to sharpen your listening skills.

The first time I became acutely aware of my listening shortcomings was during a meeting with one of my mentors, Dick Connor. Connor had a habit of taping meetings and key conversations. We would meet every couple of months to discuss a new article and identify the key points. Every time we sat down at Dick's dining room table, he would have the tape recorder and a spare tape ready. He would turn it on and then get to work.

Later I took the tape home and reviewed it. I was amazed at the number of gems and insights that came up during the discussion that I had simply forgotten. Had that tape not existed, clearly over half of the information we discussed wouldn't have been available to me. Even my prodigious note-taking didn't come close to capturing what that simple cassette tape captured.

In time, I stopped taking notes during the meetings and instead focused on the interpersonal communication. I discovered that the best time to take notes was later, while slowly reviewing the tape. Soon I developed Dick's habit without his ever suggesting it. I began taping key conversations, client interviews, and speeches. The technology is perfect—when the information is no longer of value, simply tape over. If the information is of great or lasting value, make a copy.

I learned from taping conversations that no matter how well I thought I listened, I was still obviously missing a lot and it was likely that those around me were missing a lot also.

DEFINING ACTIVE LISTENING

Active listening involves taking in the words of the speaker and seeking to grasp the facts and feeling behind them. Active listeners respond in a conversation by stating their impression of what the other person is saying. Psychotherapists have long used this technique because it reassures the patient that the therapist understands, and it encourages the person to open up.

Let's say that Travis is the president of a small research and development organization. He thinks his sales manager, Kurt, is taking on too much work, decreasing overall efficiency among the sales team. Travis is practiced in active listening. He invites Kurt into his office, asks his assistant to hold all phone calls, and offers Kurt a cup of tea (attention to those details is important in setting up an atmosphere where a useful conversation can take place). Following is a conversation between Travis and Kurt that illustrates the major points of active listening.

Travis: *Kurt, it seems as though your sales team members have been able to take it pretty easy lately, while you seem overworked. Have you noticed that?*

Kurt: *Actually, I guess I have been working a little harder than usual. I have to do everything myself though. I can't trust those guys to do things right.*

Travis: *So, you're saying that you're the only person who can handle accounts with the proper amount of care?*

Kurt: *Yes. Steven was late on delivery of two reports for our biggest client. The reports were done. Steve just didn't deliver them on time.*

Travis: *You're a little jumpy about the rest of the team because of Steven's mistake.*

Kurt: *That's right. They acted like it was no big deal.*

It's easy to see that Travis is going to get to the bottom of the problem using active listening techniques. Travis never makes suggestions for solutions. He merely repeats what he thinks Kurt meant. Paraphrasing does not imply agreement of what is being said, merely acceptance that the other person has a right to that feeling or statement.

Active listening is good for business for many reasons. Supervisors who are active listeners show that they believe their employees have experience, ideas, problems, and solutions that are worth attention. This helps subordinates gain respect for themselves and for their supervisors.

Spontaneous contributions from employees tend to increase as each person feels comfortable exposing his or her ideas before the supervisor and the work group. Cohesiveness produced by this increased comfort level can be good for profits. Research reveals that the relationship between cohesion and productivity is particularly strong.

Active listening also keeps others off the defensive, gets problems out into the open, calms down angry people, prevents mistakes made by those hearing only part of a customer's order or a supervisor's request, and establishes strong relationships.

OBSTACLES TO EFFECTIVE LISTENING

Dr. Chester L. Karrass, director of the Santa Monica, California-based Center for Effective Negotiation, which conducts negotiation seminars nationwide, offers several reasons why we don't listen as well as we could.

- We often have a lot on our minds, and it's not easy to switch gears quickly to fully absorb and participate in what is being said to us.
- We have adopted the habit of talking and interrupting too much and not letting the other party continue even when it may be to our benefit.
- We are anxious to rebut what the other person has said, and if we don't do so readily, we're afraid we may forget our point.
- We allow ourselves to be easily distracted because of the setting or environment in which the meeting takes place.
- We jump to conclusions before all the evidence has been presented or is available.
- We discount some statements because we don't place importance on the person presenting them.
- We tend to disregard information that doesn't match what we want to hear or that we don't like.

Dr. Karrass points out that the "poor listeners often drop out of a conversation with the hope that they will catch up later. This seldom happens." If you find that your mind is wandering away while listening, make a conscious (and repeated, if need be) effort to focus on the conversation.

Another key reason that we don't listen well is that the average person speaks at a rate of 125 words per minute. The average listener can process between 400 and 500 words per minute. Because we're able to think much faster than the normal speaking rate, it's easy to let our minds race ahead of the speaker, not focus on what's being said, or appear disinterested.

The faster our ability to process information, the greater the chances are to daydream or practice other bad listening habits. Good listeners use the lag time to make mental summaries of information presented and notes of ideas to pursue later without losing focus on the conversation.

Evaluate Listening Skills

The following checklist, developed by Richard C. Cupka, former director of the Institute for Leadership Education at Purdue University, will help you to evaluate your own listening habits.

- Do you give the other party a chance to talk?
- Do you interrupt while someone is making a point?
- Do you look at the speaker while he or she is talking?
- Do you impart the feeling that your time is being wasted?
- Are you constantly fidgeting with a pencil or paper?
- Do you smile at the person talking to you?
- Do you ever get the speaker off the subject?
- Are you open to new suggestions or do you stifle them?
- Do you anticipate what the other person will say next?
- Do you put the other person on the defensive when you are asked a question?
- Do you ask questions that indicate that you have not been listening?
- Do you try to out-stare the speaker?
- Do you overdo your show of attention by nodding too much or saying yes to everything?

- Do you insert humorous remarks when the other person is being serious?
- Do you frequently sneak looks at your watch or the clock while listening?

This is a tough list, and anyone who is willing to reflect honestly will undoubtedly discover several areas for improvement. The Figure 9-1 below contrasts bad and good listening:

FIGURE 9-1, TEN KEYS TO EFFECTIVE LISTENING

Ten Keys to Effective Listening	The Bad Listener	The Good Listener
1. Find areas of interest.	Tunes out dry subjects.	Seeks opportunity; asks, "What's in it for me?"
2. Judge content, not delivery.	Tunes out if delivery is poor.	Judges content, skips over delivery errors.
3. Hold your fire.	Tends to enter into argument.	Doesn't judge until comprehension is complete.
4. Listen for ideas.	Listens for facts.	Listens for central themes.
5. Be flexible.	Takes intensive notes rarely looking up.	Takes some key notes; uses other systems, depending on speaker.
6. Work at listening.	Shows no energy output; fakes attention.	Works hard; exhibits active body state.
7. Resist distractions.	Is easily distracted.	Fights or avoids distractions; knows how to concentrate.

FIGURE 9-1, CONTINUED

Ten Keys to Effective Listening	The Bad Listener	The Good Listener
8. Exercise your mind.	Resists difficult material; seeks light, easy material.	Uses heavier material as exercise for the mind.
9. Keep your mind open.	Reacts to emotional words.	Interprets color words; does not get hung up on them.
10. Capitalize on thought being faster than speech.	Tends to daydream with slow speakers.	Challenges; anticipates; mentally summarizes; weighs the evidence; listens between the lines to tone of voice.

Even if you are a great listener—and there are few—you won't reap the full benefits of listening effectively unless you let your audience know how well you have listened. How can you do this? After someone has spoken to you, ask pointed questions, reflect on something that they have said, or discuss action that you will take as a result of their message.

Following are some good tips from Arnold "Nick" Carter, a longtime vice president of the Nightingale-Conant Corporation, on what you can do to actively improve your listening capability:

- Listen for key words that give you the clue to the main thrust of what is being said.
- Control your emotions throughout the listening experience.
- Analyze what has been said, what is meant, and the thrust of the communication.
- Track logically and accurately as you listen.
- Outline as you listen to see how the pieces fit.
- Have fun listening and feeling yourself growing and understanding during the process.

YOUR NEXT CHANCE

The next time you talk to anyone, listen carefully, rather than thinking of your next statement or question. *Let* yourself be interested rather than *trying* to be interesting. When it's your turn to speak, asking such open-ended questions as, "What could be done to strengthen this report?" will encourage responses. Saying, "I need help" or "I don't know" often shows strength, not weakness.

Tape a few meetings in your office. The tapes will point out your listening shortcomings and will also help you to analyze your own communication patterns. Listen for such details as your rate of speech, stridency, and tonality. Your voice needs to be pleasant and varied enough to remain interesting.

Are your transitions logical or do you jump from one subject to the next? Do you take over the conversation? The most important question to ask yourself as you listen to the tapes is, "Was the conversation a useful exchange of ideas?" If not, try correcting some of the communication patterns you heard that were destructive to the exchange.

Remember that good listening skills take time and practice. Follow the ten keys to good listening in Figure 9-1, ask yourself the questions regarding your listening habits discussed earlier, and open your mind to what other people are saying. It could be the most important skill you'll develop in years.

CHAPTER 10

SHARPENING YOUR COMMUNICATION SKILLS

Good communication is as stimulating as
black coffee, and just as hard to sleep after.
—Anne Morrow Lindbergh

COMMUNICATION IS AN EXCHANGE—A SIMPLE BUT vital concept. Yet, all too often we approach interchanges with no consideration of how the other party will react. Our own message looms large, overshadowing the person with whom we are communicating.

Cultivating an awareness of how another person is likely to react to your communication is key to effective communication. Next, create an identification with the other person. In addition to putting that person at ease, it will open your mind to his or her perceptions and reactions—a vital part of communication.

Donald J. Moine, of Redondo Beach, California, is a psychologist who heads his own sales and management training firm. Dr. Moine compared the sales techniques of high-achieving and mediocre salespeople. He found that top sales personnel instinctively match, with hypnotic effect, the customer's voice tone, rhythm, volume, and speech rate. Career marketers, take note!

"The good salesman or saleswoman matches the customer's posture, body language, and mood," explains Moine. "If the customer is slightly depressed, the salesperson shares that feeling and acknowledges that he or she has been feeling a little down lately. In essence, the top sales producer becomes a sophisticated biofeedback mechanism, sharing and reflecting the customer's reality— even to the point of breathing with the customer."

The technique works because "hypnotic pacing" helps establish trust and rapport. It does not work as a gesture, however. Anything other than an honest attempt to understand the other person and his or her frame of reference in a particular situation will be seen as mimicking, which will decrease trust.

Whether writing a letter, speaking with a coworker, or calling a client, consider that person's likely mood and reaction. What effect is your message likely to have? How can you phrase that message for maximum benefit?

Higher Levels of Communication

According to Lyman Steil, Ph.D., an authority on communication, we all communicate with each other on four levels.

- The first level is small talk, or informal conversation.
- The second level is catharsis—venting feelings and sharing problems and frustrations.
- The third level is the exchange of information, the level most of us use during the typical business day—talking over strategies or passing on facts.
- Persuasion is the fourth level. People generally warm up to this level, beginning with small talk and going on to level two or three, finally trying to convince you to change your mind or sell you on an idea.

In the following part of this chapter, the primary concern is honing your skills at levels two and three. Later, we focus on level four because adeptness in persuading others will be the most helpful level to you in your career marketing efforts.

ENHANCING YOUR COMMUNICATION SKILLS

Establishing eye contact is vital to opening up a line of dialogue with another person. Think back to uncomfortable situations you've been in during your career. Were you looking down or away from the person speaking? Was the other person constantly focusing at a point somewhere over your shoulder? Staring at someone is often taken as a threat or an insult, but a direct, clear gaze is important.

Notice people who try to get your attention, such as political workers at the entrances to polls or volunteers for charity during Christmas or other holidays. Before they say one word, they seek to establish eye contact. Looking down, hunching your shoulders, and hurrying away will usually dissuade them from attempting a conversation. If they catch your eye, however, it's nearly certain you'll listen to what they say.

Not surprisingly, Salvation Army "Santas" claim that they almost always get a donation if they make eye contact with pedestrians. Salespeople who use eye contact with customers generate more and larger sales. The same goes for working in the business world. Managers and executives who use their eyes when talking with their staff open up communications, get more work done, and rise faster in their careers.

If you're leading a meeting, get there in time either to talk to or establish eye contact with and nod to all the people attending. They will feel more like participating and you will have the opportunity to gauge their moods.

MAXIMIZING USE OF THE TELEPHONE

You wouldn't think of walking into someone's office and starting a conversation without knocking first. Yet people do that every day on the telephone. Always give the person the option to call you back later if it's not a good time.

Since you can't see the other person, which generally accounts for a great deal of information during a conversation, ask extra questions about how the person feels concerning what you're saying. When you call an office and the person isn't in, leave a complete message. Give your name, title, organization, and a brief explanation of why you are calling.

Joe Stumpf, an automated sales training specialist, offers many techniques for professional use of the telephone. Here are some examples:

1. Answer the phone on the second or third ring, if possible. Your goal when answering the phone is making the caller feel important and comfortable, and you have about 15 seconds to make a lasting first impression.
2. Never start your phone presentation with an apology. You lose all control and positioning.
3. Answer your phone with enthusiasm. It's positive and contagious. Place a mirror next to your phone. Before you answer, look in the mirror and say, "I answer my phone with enthusiasm."
4. Smile when you talk. You sound happier.
5. Develop a sincere and positive attitude. People know when you're faking it.
6. Speak slowly. The normal rate of speech is 150 words per minute on the phone. Slow down to 100 words per minute.
7. Have empathy. Listen. Let them know you understand.
8. Don't interrupt.
9. Take notes. This will help you remember important points.
10. Listen for the overtones.

11. Use the caller's name. It is, for him or her, the sweetest sound in language.
12. Be proud of yourself and your position. How you feel about yourself is heard in your voice.
13. Pause!
14. Show you're grateful and appreciative. Say, "Thank you."

This is a long list, and you're not likely to master it soon, but if you follow only a handful of the tips, your phone skills will improve immediately.

THE NONVERBAL CLUES OF CONVERSATION

When speaking in person rather than on the phone, you can, of course, read a person's nonverbal clues. Any time that interpersonal communication takes place, there are nonverbal clues in the conversation. The effective career marketer becomes aware of and constantly monitors various body language signals, such as personal space, posture, and gestures.

1. **Personal space.** How far away does the other party stand? A normal space zone between two people in business is four to twelve feet. Still, everyone's space zone may differ. Monitor any changes during a conversation or over the course of many conversations that may indicate an attitude change in the person.
2. **Posture.** Is the other person standing tall (exhibiting confidence) or slouching (possibly indicating defeat, depression, or lack of confidence)? Notice your own posture when speaking to different people in your office. Do you stand differently when talking to your supervisor versus a coworker? Your goal is to present impeccable posture every time!
3. **Gestures.** Are the person's gestures consistent with the spoken message? If your boss praises your work while turning away from you to look elsewhere, the messages are

inconsistent. You'll be safe to take the nonverbal gesture—looking away—as the more accurate one, since we're in more conscious control of our verbal, rather than nonverbal, statements.

Whether or not you seek to be, you are communicating all day long, especially when you're at work. By becoming more aware of this dynamic process and the verbal and nonverbal clues that you send to bosses, coworkers, and the office staff, you can better position yourself to relay the type of message you choose.

Level Four—Persuasion

More than 100 years ago, author Robert Louis Stevenson said, "Everyone lives by selling something." Could that apply to *everyone*? Surely not to a newborn baby, for instance, or to a nun. Or could it? A newborn baby sells love, affection, and hope for the future to parents, relatives, and siblings. A nun sells the love of God, love of humanity, and the spirit of brotherhood and sisterhood for all. If you are married, you have already made the ultimate sale—convincing your spouse that it would be in his or her best interests to share a life with you.

What about selling at the workplace? One partner with a Big Six accounting firm observed that between any two people, at any given time, one is selling something to the other. This is a profound realization and one that can easily be misunderstood.

Whether you're with your boss, a coworker, production staff, a member of your family, or a friend, hundreds if not thousands of "sales" are occurring continuously. Shall we meet at 9 P.M. or 10 P.M.? Does the report need to include the extra exhibit? Do we choose this restaurant or that? To resolve such questions, one person undoubtedly influences or obtains agreements from the other.

Even if the actual position you presently hold doesn't remotely involve formal or designated responsibility for selling, you will nevertheless advance in your career by improving your salesmanship.

BRIMMING WITH ENTHUSIASM

Dale Carnegie probably said it best in the 1930s when he remarked, "Enthusiasm is contagious." The enthusiasm you have for your current task, projects on which you work, your job, your organization, and your community, *is* contagious. When you become excited and enthusiastic about what you're doing, you'll more readily gain the interest and participation of others. Approach the same task with a "who-gives-a-darn" attitude and absolutely no one will want to help you.

Have you ever noticed that some of the most successful people that you know are motivated by powerful slogans and phrases? My late father, who was the vice principal of a junior high school, used to win people over the second they entered his office. His walls were filled with pictures of great Americans such as Abraham Lincoln and Martin Luther King Jr. and slogans and phrases that he would sometimes refer to and draw upon when working with a troubled adolescent. Simply entering his office was an uplifting experience.

I suggest that you glance through Bartlett's familiar quotations, similar books, or CD-Roms. Slogans and phrases can empower and help to energize us. I keep several such books by my desk, and whenever I find enthusiasm or energy waning, or I need to get charged up to close a deal, I spend a minute or two with these powerful passages. Here are three of my favorites:

> *All men dream, but not equally. They who dream by night in the dusty recesses of their minds wake in the day to find that it is vanity; but the dreamers of the day are the dangerous men, for they act their dream with open eyes, to make it possible.* —T.E.Lawrence ("Lawrence of Arabia")

> *In this culture you have to define yourself very strongly and clearly or people won't see you . . . I have dreamed my own self into being. If we collectively dream a future, together, we can obtain it.* —Alice Walker

Enlightened men living in a democracy readily discover that nothing can confine them, hold them, or force them to be content with their present lot. —Alexis de Tocqueville

Review such a phrase or slogan, any that may appeal to you, before you have to make a presentation, or when you've made an unpopular decision that you know to be right, or simply because you want to. Even the most enthusiastic among us often suffer some "down time." Powerful statements tend to recharge our batteries.

IT ALL STARTS IN YOUR MIND

Irrespective of your position in your present organization, to whom you have to report, and whom you need to influence to get ahead, selling, as we have discussed, is an essential part of your career success. All top earners in professional selling agree that the sale, any sale, starts in the seller's *mind*. When *you* are firmly convinced regarding what path to take, what strategy to follow, then you are ready to effectively convince others.

Abraham Lincoln was once asked by a student what it would take to become a lawyer. "Young man," said Lincoln, "if you are firmly convinced that you are going to become a lawyer, then you are already halfway there." So it is with your sales effort.

One young entrepreneur from southern California experienced eight years of continued failure, as one bank after another continued to reject his loan application for an innovative recreational project that he had conceived. At one point, this "dreamer" had to declare bankruptcy, but in the end his selling effort prevailed. His name was Walt Disney. Today, more people have visited Disneyland and Disney World than the population of the United States.

HYPE IS HOLLOW

The biggest! The greatest! The newest! The fastest! The best!

As a consumer you probably stay away from products that make too many claims like those. And they don't work so well in the office either. The late David H. Sandler, a sales seminar trainer, believed that contrary to popular conceptions, the most influential and effective salespeople sold softly. The marks of a "super" salesperson, according to Sandler, included:

- Bringing up objections before the other party thinks of them.
- Concentrating on what will sell the idea while not trying to overimpress.
- Spending the first part of the meeting finding out about the other party's problems.
- Spending much of the meeting time getting the other party to suggest how the problem might be solved.
- Making a presentation tailored to the other party's needs.

Whether or not you've ever considered yourself a salesman or saleswoman, consider yourself one now. Over the years, selling has taken on a rather negative connotation. Yet, it's selling that turns a depressed economy around, and it's selling that enables your organization to continue to exist.

CHAPTER 11

THE CONFIDENCE TO SUCCEED

Everybody thinks of changing humanity and nobody thinks of changing himself.
—Leo Tolstoy

WHAT IS IT ABOUT SELF-CONFIDENT PEOPLE that is so attractive? Self-confident people radiate power and health. Hence, others want to be around them and be like them. Self-confidence, fortunately, is a skill you can practice! The concept gets little notice sometimes because people who don't have self-confidence confuse it with egotism. On the contrary, it's most attractive because self-confident people make other people feel confident.

A self-confident person walks into a job interview knowing that he has the skills and knowledge to handle the position being offered. A self-confident person asks to be promoted based on an assurance that the promotion is deserved because of past work. Self-confidence comes from feeling that you deserve to *have* and *be* what you want.

SELF-CONFIDENCE: VITAL TO YOUR CAREER

Self-confidence is a prerequisite to success and happiness since performance is often based on attitude rather than aptitude.

Success or failure can become a self-fulfilling prophecy. This is particularly true in the area of self-marketing. If you want a promotion or a raise but aren't confident that you deserve it, you're likely to let your doubts get in your way. You may be reluctant to directly approach those in charge of promotions. Or, you might couch your request in a vague manner, using such terms as "maybe," "if," and "sometime."

A confident person applying for a new job writes a cover letter that states, "I will do x, y, and z for your company," and "I look forward to hearing from you." Such statements imply right from the start that the applicant expects to be interviewed and hired. The less confident applicant couches the correspondence in terms of, "I could do x, y, and z for your company," and "I hope to hear from you." These statements imply doubt. In the mind of whoever reads the letter, that doubt easily extends to the applicant's appropriateness for the job. Confidence means taking a positive approach—an approach that has a way of influencing other people.

If you expect to do well at any particular endeavor—from performing a task on the job to gaining social acceptance outside the job—you're likely to do far better than you would if you expect mediocrity or failure. Teachers have known for years that students who are told they are progressing well in spelling, math, or whatever tend to achieve more than students who are told they are having problems. Doubts compromise your effectiveness, and self-doubt makes it unlikely that you can effectively market yourself. It's like trying to sell a product you don't believe in. You can't commit yourself to it wholeheartedly.

HOW TO LOOK BETTER IN A HURRY

Self-confidence increases your attractiveness to other people, and that, in turn, also can increase your effectiveness. So much of what we do—at work and outside work—is done with or through other people. When they sense that you're confident, they want to be around you, support you, and even be like you. They "go to bat" for you and generally assist you in being as effective as you can be. It makes them feel good to be around someone who has a positive, enthusiastic, "can do" attitude. On the other hand, people tend to avoid someone who's continually worried, self-doubting, and skeptical.

Peace of mind and contentment with life follow on the heels of acceptance of yourself, which then leads to acceptance of others. Conversely, many forms of destructive behavior are due to low self-confidence. For instance, a mid-level manager at a high technology firm constantly befriended new employees, only to spread rumors about them later. This man, unsure about his own place in the company, felt it necessary to sabotage the reputation of new employees. Such behavior only destroyed his own position in the long run.

Confidence seems to create a resiliency that allows you to bounce back from failures. Positive self-esteem provides a reservoir of inner strength—a constant that is not dependent upon others and the situations in which you find yourself. Conversely, lack of self-esteem saps your energy with worries about acceptance and accomplishments, creating a downward spiral when those worries do begin to hamper your effectiveness.

INCREASING SELF-CONFIDENCE

You're *not* stuck with your present degree of confidence. If you've ever found yourself thinking, "I'm not a confident person," you're wrong. Confidence isn't handed out at birth; it can be developed. Of course, developing it is hard work, even lonely work. When you begin to work on becoming more self-confident, you may not get a lot of support from others. Do it anyway; they'll come around sooner than you think.

Take a good look at the root of your lack of self-confidence. Where does it come from? In what situations is it most problematic? In what situations do things seem a little better? Finding the answers to such questions can help you dispel personal myths, point out positive occurrences, and begin a realistic program to build your confidence.

In my case, I spent years convinced that I wasn't as smart as a lot of other people. Even though my record in high school was way above average, I felt that I could never compete with my brilliant friends. Until I was about thirty years old, I was certain that truly brilliant people, like some of those I had known in high school, were not at all uncommon, and, of course, I would never quite achieve that lofty status. I finally realized that my brightest school friends were not actually representative of the entire population as a whole. Simply understanding the roots of my lack of confidence—and dispelling some myths about it—bolstered my own confidence enormously.

It helps to determine the exact situations in which you feel more or less confident. Don't worry about them, write them down; and continue by writing a plan of action for improving the situation. For example, your action plan might look like this:

I feel most confident when . . .
I feel least confident when . . .
Things I can do to improve a situation of low confidence are . . .

Here's how one person completed the above:

I feel most confident when I know I am wearing clothes appropriate to the situation, when I am physically fit, and when I am among people I know well. I feel least confident when I am among strangers and when I feel I have taken on more than I can achieve in a given time frame. To improve a situation that instills low confidence, I need to look and feel my best, to be highly organized in my work, and to operate under the assumption that everybody suffers a certain amount of discomfort in a room full of strangers.

You also learn about your personal level of confidence by examining how you act and react at home, at work, alone, and in the company of others. The questionnaire used by author Sam Horn in Figure 11-1 is designed to help you pinpoint situations that may be precursors to feelings of low self-confidence. Indicate true or false after each statement (Add a little explanation if you like).

Figure 11-1, Confidence Questionnaire

_____ I tend to complete tasks successfully that I wholeheartedly attack.

_____ I feel uncomfortable about the amount of formal education I've had.

_____ I check and recheck to make sure I have done things even though I know they were done.

_____ I have frequently wished that I could act more spontaneously more often.

_____ I have no qualms about meeting new males or females.

_____ Sometimes it seems that everyone is seeking my opinion on something.

_____ The one word that best describes me in my childhood and to some extent today is *inadequate*.

_____ I have always regretted that I could not live up to my parents' expectations for me.

_____ I get enough feedback at work to know that I am performing satisfactorily.

_____ I have often found myself thinking self-condemning thoughts.

_____ I feel that I don't have the right to criticize anyone for anything because I have my own failings.

_____ I feel a sense of accomplishment from my work.

_____ Basically, I accept and respect myself for the person I am.

_____ I often find myself worrying about what others are thinking about me.

It isn't difficult to review your answers and see where some problems might lie. For example, if you answered false to "I get enough feedback at work . . . ", you may sense a lack of confidence at work that stems from ambiguity about your performance. In this case, the remedy may be in taking the initiative to ask for feedback. This is particularly likely to boost your confidence, because people performing badly generally get plenty of feedback.

Another example: If you answered true to "I feel uncomfortable about the amount of formal education . . .," your lack of confidence in this area may mean that you expect to achieve less than your educated colleagues, and, therefore, *do* achieve less. But remember—many great achievers throughout history had little education.

THE ART OF CONFIDENCE-BUILDING

Beyond analyzing the sources and situations concerning your level of confidence, there are some specific strategies you can adopt and steps you can take to learn and practice confidence-building:

Stay focused. Practicing self-confidence won't change you into wonder-woman or superman overnight—or ever. Self-confidence will allow you to make the best of what you *can* do.

Know what you're good at. Your confidence may be so low that it seems you do nothing well. But stop and think about even the small things that you do each day—from organizing your mail to meeting self-imposed deadlines for routine chores. You may be surprised to find some abilities and positive features that you haven't given ample credit to in the past. Making a list works well. You'll find that by emphasizing the positive, you'll gain confidence to work on the less positive.

Make yourself happy. Extending yourself to impress others runs counter to the idea of confidence. You may need to spend more time doing things simply because *you* want to do them and they make you feel good. These are the activities in which you're most likely to succeed and that are most likely to bolster your confidence when they go well.

Look for small wins. Maybe you didn't get that promotion, but pat yourself on the back for getting asked your opinion in a meeting or for completing that report ahead of schedule. Don't figure all is lost if the big accomplishments elude you for now. If everything seems to be falling apart in one area of your life, look for achievements in another.

Reward yourself. Enjoy your successes. Celebrating success helps you take the focus off your mistakes. When you finish a budget or report on deadline, take yourself—and others—out to a movie. When you get some overdue positive feedback, treat yourself to a lunch hour at a museum or buy yourself a book you've been wanting. Let other people know you are celebrating and that they're important enough to you that you want them to share.

Learn from failure. Don't let mistakes drag you down by dwelling on them. Instead, regard them as lessons—stepping stones that give you a higher vantage point for better knowledge and wisdom. Be glad that you've learned that lesson and won't make that mistake again. But, give yourself permission to make some mistakes and to be a little less than perfect.

Sound confident. Practice using positive terms in conversation. For example, despite some concerns you may have, simply say, "Yes, we will get that done," or, "I can get it finished on time." Your confidence will likely lead to a better chance of accomplishing what you've set out to do. Practice speaking without saying, "but," "maybe," "if," "I'm not sure," and other qualifiers.

Look the part. No matter how you feel today, dress and groom yourself as you would on a day when you were feeling on top of the world. Remind yourself to stand as if you want to be an inch taller and walk with a firm, purposeful stride. When you keep your head up and maintain good eye contact, those around you act more interested and confident in you. And that, in turn, will build *your* confidence.

Initiate conversations. It's not easy to start talking to people you don't know, but force yourself to do it. We all start as strangers.

What's the worst that can happen? They are unlikely to turn and run away or to act insulted or angry. Starting a conversation with a stranger at a conference or a party will build your confidence, because they will generally respond with interest and gratitude. People will view you and treat you as a self-confident person.

Prepare discussions. Play through any upcoming scheduled meetings, interviews, or conversations ahead of time. This prepares you to handle most obstacles that could arise. Make some notes to yourself about topics, questions, and responses. If you're at a loss for words in social situations, make some mental notes about all the topics of "small talk" about which you could ask questions or initiate discussions. These could range from the weather to the front page news. What you say may not be as important as the fact that you are able to say something with confidence.

Imitate self-confident people. Identify the people around you who have a good degree of self-confidence and observe them. I find this technique to be effective. Is it how they work, what they say, how they carry themselves? Select one small behavior at a time and try to emulate it. Dr. Judy Kuriansky, a radio talk show host and author, says imitation is essential to learning. She notes that if you are attracted to self-confidence in others, it's likely that you have the capacity for greater personal self-confidence. The qualities we admire and envy in others usually reflect our own undeveloped capacities.

Experiment with roles. In the privacy of your home, preferably in front of a mirror, act out the self-confident attitudes and manners that a confident person would show the world. A friend of mine once related that he has eight different hats, ranging from a baseball cap to a Texas ten-gallon hat. Every morning, he puts on a different hat depending on what challenges he will face that day. Then he pictures meeting those challenges while he looks at himself in the mirror. Hey, use whatever works for you!

Increasing your self-confidence is primarily a matter of finding out what makes you feel good about yourself, and then practicing these behavior patterns. It means assuring yourself and others that you have made and will continue to make some highly worthwhile accomplishments—without shrugging off any accomplishments as too insignificant to count. As you display this attitude more and more, others will soon increase their confidence in you. And that will lead to even greater self-confidence for you.

PART IV

ACCELERATING YOUR PROGRESS

WHAT YOU READ AND HOW YOU READ IT

For him who has no concentration, there is no tranquillity.

—Bhagavad Gita

READING IS A VITAL COMPONENT OF YOUR CAREER marketing effort. Much of what you know about your career and your industry you learn from reading. Indeed, to become an authority in your field, you need to ingest certain basic types of information. Mastering your reading will make this ongoing task less onerous.

Most successful executives read and seek out industry data to help them support their views or to form new ones. They manage their professional reading as if their careers depended on it—because they do. However, as business professionals, we face a daily avalanche of reading materials, Internet information, intranet news, subscriptions, e-mail, and junk mail. It's seemingly impossible to maintain a reading and information intake schedule for work-related requirements. Is keeping pace hopeless or is there a way out of this information overload morass?

A FRIGHTENING PACE

In speaking to supervisors and business professionals throughout the country, you soon realize that professional reading is regarded as an important component of the job and career, yet there is seemingly no time, or precious little, that can be allotted for it. In addition, the number of quality business, career, and management publications has more than doubled since the early-1990s, only adding to the confusion over what to read and when to read it, and that was before you add in the Internet, e-mail, the rise of newsletters, and the explosive growth of direct mail.

WHAT TYPE OF INFORMATION DO YOU NEED?

Redefine, or perhaps more accurately define, the type of information to which you *need* to be exposed, and what type of information can be readily discarded or ignored. I started to realize that unless I figured out what I must read, what I might read, and what I like to read, I would remain hopelessly flooded.

Key publications and sources of information that supply you directly with what you need to know are to be preferred over passive sources—those publications such as the daily paper, general interest periodicals, and much direct-mail material that take up more time than they're worth, and merely interesting websites, e-mail, come-ons, and other enticers.

If giving up the daily paper, dropping some of your favorite subscriptions, or greatly reducing the number of websites you've bookmarked leaves you cold, take heart. Everyone needs some pleasure reading. The question is, how much and when?

If you're skeptical as to how much time can be saved or allocated for active reading, test yourself over the next thirty days. Briefly skim the paper or read only the Sunday edition or a weekly news magazine. Listen to intelligent radio and TV reports. Set limits as to how much time you'll cruise the Internet. Once you give up cover-to-cover reading of the daily paper, for example, you will probably wonder why you ever developed that habit in the first place.

VITAL SKILLS: SKIMMING AND SCANNING

If you did not master "skimming and scanning" in high school or college, it's not too late to learn. *Skimming* involves perusing the first one or two sentences of a paragraph within an article to see if the information in the paragraph is relevant to your immediate quest. You can also use skimming when you're simultaneously confronted with several journals or periodicals. The basic payoff to skimming is that it enables you to quickly determine whether or not to invest more time in the article or the publication.

Scanning is a technique used with large volume materials. Often I have to research several books, periodicals, or websites for the purpose of extracting key information. Scanning enables me to effectively handle the task quickly. Scanning involves reviewing the table of contents, index or site map, list of charts and exhibits, and occasional paragraph leads to determine what, if any, material is of interest. The availability of high-speed photocopiers and printers greatly facilitates the scanning process since you can directly capture a hard copy of whatever items you may need.

You can enhance both of these techniques by speed reading. By moving a pencil under the text as quickly as your eyes can follow, yet still reading the words, you can almost double your skimming and scanning rates. If you enroll in an executive level speed-reading course, you can read even faster than that.

MAKE YOUR DESK YOUR READING POST

Virtually every kind of professional-type reading is more effectively undertaken sitting at a desk rather than a chair, couch, or even a table. At a desk you have ready access to your PC, fax, fax/modem, printer, and copier. Also, you're near your stationery, envelopes, scissors, pens, pencils, ruler, and all other office supplies that enable you to clip, tear, send for, save, and file what you've read. I find it useful to start a "clip" file of articles that interest me even if they have no immediate link to what I'm doing, and to review this file periodically to see what ideas take shape.

Many professionals, surprisingly, feel guilty about reading at the office. The guilt, in part, stems from the fact that reading at the desk doesn't appear to be productive; it doesn't cause one to perspire. Many people erroneously believe that if they aren't engaging in some form of motion, they're not being productive.

Your professional reading is an important part of your job and you *deserve* the right to read at your desk. However, even if there is no stigma attached to the act, you may still find it difficult in the midst of the office hustle and bustle. If you haven't done so before, now may be a good time to allocate a certain number of hours per week for uninterrupted professional reading at the office. Many professionals choose to do this early in the morning or late in the day. The time is not important. What is important is that you don't kid yourself into thinking that you can read, absorb, and apply important data or information while surrounded by noise.

YOU CAN DELEGATE READING

You may not have considered it previously, but a stack of periodicals you've been wanting to get through, those key chapters in the latest book, the several website locations (URLs) you've jotted down, or those reports that have been piling up often don't have to be read by *you*. If you have any employees who report to you, some of your reading can be delegated to your staff. All that's necessary to effectively delegate some of your reading workload is to provide clear instructions as to what you're looking for and how you want it presented.

Perhaps you only need to have a few key paragraphs underlined. Maybe you need a one-page listing of pros and cons on a certain issue or procedure, or maybe you only need to have a printout of the opening screen to a key website.

USING ONLINE SOURCES

More people are spending more time doing more of their reading on the web. Why? According to *What Makes People Click,* by NetSmart, 97 percent of users want to be better informed, 81 percent to research product and service information, with a large percentage becoming buyers, and 57 percent for fun.

More people are also relying on a hierarchy of bookmarks to help them easily return to favorite sources of information. A survey of 17,000 users by Georgia Institute of Technology revealed that 18 percent of users bookmark one to ten items, 39 percent bookmark eleven to fifty items, 19 percent bookmark fifty-one to one hundred items, and 19 percent bookmark more than one hundred.

To find a product, service, or general information on the Web, many people tap one or more of the online search engines and request a key word search. Some search engines scour the Web locating and indexing new sites as they appear. Others, like Yahoo (http://www.yahoo.com), list only those sites that are submitted to them.

Some search engines index only home pages; others the entire site. Most people don't realize that each search engine operates differently. When you find one that allows you to navigate comfortably, stay with it. I like http://www.hotbot.com for its simplicity. Another notable site is http://www.NLsearch.com. Beyond serving as free search engines, NLsearch.com offers the full text articles of more than 6000 journals and magazines. Article abstracts are free while the full text is available for a nominal fee.

The key to finding precisely what you want is using multiple word searches. Nearly every search engine allows you to use quote marks (" ") to identify key phrases and more quickly hone in on the desired information. Most engines also allow you to place a plus sign (+) in front of words that you want to have included in the information you're seeking, and a minus sign (-) to exclude words. So, if you're looking for information on advancing in your career in the music industry, it might help to exclude phrases like "rock star" and "heavy metal."

If you're seeking to gain access to many search engines, visit Site Promoter (http://www.sitepromoter.com), which contains links to the top fifty promotional search engines, as well as links to a secondary set of one hundred general business promotional engines.

SERVICES THAT EASE YOUR READING

In regard to non-web information intake, you can reduce your reading time by employing one or more of several excellent book review services. SoundView Executive Book Summaries, for example, capsulates leading management and business books into four- to eight-page summaries and offers new titles every month. Contact:

SoundView Executive Book Summaries
3 Pond Lane
Middlebury, VT 05753-1164
800-521-1227

Another service is the Book Notes at the Breathing Space Resource Center, my own website. More than 100 books are summarized and available for review. For more information, visit:

Book Notes
Breathing Space Resource Center
http://www.BreathingSpace.com

Also, check the current edition of *Literary Marketplace* (published by R. R. Bowker & Company) in the reference section of any library for a complete listing of book review publications.

NEWSLETTERS

Newsletters can be a valuable source of information. They are published by government agencies, industry groups, associations, political groups, and virtually every corporation. The *Oxbridge Directory of Newsletters* lists several thousand newsletters, arranged by functional area. The *National Trade and Professional Association Directory of the United States* (NTPA) indicates which of the thousands of associations listed maintain a newsletter. The *Newsletter Yearbook* is also a valuable guide. By accessing these directories and others that your local librarian may suggest, you can gain access to late-breaking news and information of concern to your business and industry.

There are also many management, communications, and business newsletters that effectively scan what you may have chosen to scan yourself. Two are listed below.

Bottom Line/Tomorrow
Box 2614
55 Railroad Avenue
Greenwich, CT 06836-2614
203-625-5223

Communication Briefings
1101 King Street, #110
Alexandria, VA 22314-2944
703-548-3800

NEWSLETTER DIRECTORIES

If you're interested in reviewing a wide range of industry newsletters, the following directories can be helpful.

Standard Periodical Directory lists more than 72,000 magazines, journals, newsletters, directories, house organs, and association publications throughout the United States and Canada:

Standard Periodical Directory
Oxbridge Communications, Inc.
150 Fifth Avenue, Suite 302
New York, NY 10011
212-741-0231

Oxbridge lists 5,500 newsletters in the U.S. and Canada.

Oxbridge Directory of Newsletters
Oxbridge Communications, Inc.
150 Fifth Avenue, Suite 302
New York, NY 10011
212-741-0231

The *National Directory of Newsletters and Reporting Services* lists thousands of newsletters issued by commercial and noncommercial publishers:

National Directory of Newsletters and Reporting Services
Gale Research Company
Book Tower
Detroit, MI 48226
313-961-2242

The *Hudson's Subscription Newsletter Directory* lists several thousand newsletters offered through subscription:

Hudson's Subscription Newsletter Directory
44 West Market Street
Rhinebeck, NY 12572
914-876-2081

SCOPING OUT MAGAZINES

Bacon's Magazine Directory is a gold mine when it comes to identifying key magazines (such as those read by your clients or your organization's CEO). It presents more than 12,000 periodicals, laid out by industry with highly descriptive contact and editorial information on each publication:

> *Bacon's Magazine Directory*
> Bacon's Information, Inc.
> 332 S. Michigan Avenue
> Chicago, IL 60604
> 312-922-2400

The appendices to this book also provide you with rosters of key career-advancing information sources, including magazines and journals, newsletters, and key directories.

LISTENING TO LEARN

Your reading time can be further reduced by using your ears. Subscription cassette services such as Audio-Tech, Newstrack Executive Tape Service, and Listen & Live greatly accelerate your information gathering capability. Audio-Tech, for example, features book excerpts and condensation of leading business books—all presented in an enjoyable format.

The Newstrack Executive Tape Service abstracts and summarizes, on tape, key articles from leading business and management publications. Listen & Live Audio offers a variety of programs to stimulate your thinking. For further information:

> Audio-Tech Business Book Summaries
> 825 75th Street, Suite C
> Hinsdale, IL 60521
> 800-776-1910

Newstrack Executive Tape Service
47 S. Broadway
Pitman, NJ 08071
800-334-5771

Listen & Live Audio
P.O. Box 817
Roseland, NJ 07068
201-798-3830

Great Minds of the Western Intellectual Tradition
The Teaching Company
7405 Alban Station Court #107
Springfield, VA 22150-2318
1-800-832-2412

Many other tape cassette services are available. Consult the business reference librarian at your local library.

READERS ARE LEADERS

In summary, the old slogan that your grammar school teacher posted on the wall has been true all along—*Readers are Leaders*. When you adopt ways to absorb more vital information in less time, you'll have more time to lead.

CHAPTER 13

CAREER MARKETING AND WRITING SKILLS

An intellectual is a man who takes more words than necessary to tell more than he knows.
—Dwight D. Eisenhower

LISTENING AND READING ARE AMONG THE MOST important skills to support your career marketing efforts, and writing is not far behind. There are standard written materials or tools to prepare to support your overall marketing efforts, such as a biography, news releases, articles, and fact sheets. As you'll see, each is a vital tool in making yourself well-known in your organization, industry, and the community at large.

THE UPDATED BIOGRAPHY

A biography (or bio) is not a resume. A resume is useful for landing a new job or preparing proposals, but it's inappropriate in career marketing. A biography differs from a resume in that the biography is written in the third person as if someone were talking about you; it's not necessarily organized by chronology or function; and it is composed in an upbeat, lively, but authoritative manner. Take a look at my biography below:

FIGURE 13 -1, THE BIO

Jeff Davidson, based in Chapel Hill, North Carolina, is a leading authority on 21st century lifestyle and career strategies. In strong demand as a speaker, Jeff offers dynamic learning keynotes and seminar presentations, combining outstanding high-content with humor, flair, and inspiration, leaving his audiences supercharged and ready for action. Frequently quoted or featured in *USA Today*, *Washington Post*, and *Los Angeles Times*, and on hundreds of talk shows, a worldwide audience has found Jeff's 25 books and 3300 articles to be enlightening, entertaining, and life changing. His book, *Breathing Space*, is a ground-breaking text that will show you how to avoid racing the clock and gain more control over each day. His website (http://www.BreathingSpace.com) offers a substantial array of resources for career professionals, including daily and weekly tips, articles, quizzes, and book summaries.

Jeff has spoken in almost every industry from aviation to zoology, and has addressed individuals in administration, banking, education, finance, government, health care, manufacturing, retailing, and wholesaling. He has also addressed charitable organizations, executive round tables, and partner's programs. His client list includes many companies among the Fortune 500, and national and international associations and organizations. To book Jeff for your next meeting, call him directly at 800-735-1994.

If this bio is truncated by, say, a magazine editor, readers can still find me because of the order of the information presented.

When and where do you use a biography? Bios accompany any articles that you write, press releases about you, and any other information that you send when in contact with members of the media. Whenever someone requests information about you, other than as part of a job search, send your biography rather than your resume. To submit a resume when a biography is called for is a strong indication to the receiving party that you're not adept at career marketing.

My bio is constructed primarily to draw attention to my speaking and consulting services, and secondarily to focus on my books and tapes. Later on, when we discuss getting on radio and TV (Chapter 21), you'll find that your bio can also be used by media hosts, whereas a resume cannot be.

PRESS RELEASES

Years ago, I discovered the press or news release. Originally, I didn't realize that the pictures and little blurbs that appear in the paper each night about local dentists, lawyers, and business executives were submitted by them. I actually believed that there was a roving reporter seeking out tidbits from the business and professional community!

Most people simply don't realize that the media needs them. Newspapers are constantly looking for stories and press releases to fill their pages. Looking in the papers and seeing what others had submitted made me realize that nearly everything I was doing could also be worked into a news release.

A good news release contains information organized according to the five W's: who, what, where, when, and why (plus how). It is written in the "inverted pyramid" fashion; the most important information is presented first and the small details at the bottom. The release has to be easy to read and snappy; don't make any sentences too long or it will lose the editor right from the start. Models of successful news releases—those that I've published—are far more instructive than explanations. See Chapter 18, "Be Your Own Press Agent," for samples of published news releases.

PUBLISHING ARTICLES

Writing articles for publication is a proactive strategy for marketing your career (discussed in greater detail in Chapter 17, "Breaking into Print"). If you've ever considered writing an article but hesitated, be assured that it's not as difficult as you think. Most publications routinely edit your material. They're far more interested in receiving interesting themes and concepts submitted by people with the right qualifications.

Regardless of your field, you undoubtedly have information that will be of interest to your peers or clients. Don't make the common mistake of thinking, "Who would want to read something written by me?" That's a defeatist and unrealistic attitude. With thousands of magazines, newspapers, journals, and newsletters in print, more than two million bylined articles appear in the United States alone each year. A significant number of those are by first-time authors.

ASSEMBLING A FACT SHEET

Fact sheets have been successfully used by businesses who want to emphasize a particular product or service in a simple, cost-effective way. They can also be used on the personal level to support your overall career-marketing efforts. A fact sheet is a one-page list of data about yourself, a topic on which you are an expert, or the product or service you offer. Fact sheets can also be in question-and-answer format. Fact sheets are particularly useful for a high-gear self-marketing strategy such as getting on radio and TV. The fact sheet represents an important element of a media or press kit.

FIGURE 13-2, THE FACT SHEET

Jack Cohen . . .
Some Background Information

JACK COHEN
PRESIDENT OF SALES DYNAMICS INSTITUTE

Jack Cohen is currently an instructor in the marketing department at the University of Baltimore, where he teaches personal selling. As the director of Sales Dynamics Institute, he conducts its regularly scheduled sales skills training workshops, specializing in the SDI Selling System and the selling techniques and management strategies necessary to use this new, innovative, and relevant selling style.

Since 1951, he has been a specialist in marketing, selling-skills training, sales communications, management consulting, and marketing-support systems. He is an author, professional speaker, and seminar leader who has lectured for the academic and business communities in colleges, conventions, banquets, and workshops for multi-level audiences.

For fourteen years, he served as a corporate officer and the director of marketing for a prominent, publicly-owned company with divisions in five mid-Atlantic states employing 80 salespersons who produce more than $50M.

DICTATION EQUIPMENT AND
VOICE RECOGNITION SOFTWARE

As a supervisor, project manager, author, and professional speaker, I've discovered that when it comes to writing longhand, dictating to a secretary, or even using my own word processor, the difference between those methods and using portable dictation equipment is akin to walking up stairs versus taking the elevator in a skyscraper.

Once you become familiar with dictation equipment (whether hand-held or pocket dictation or voice recognition systems), and the convenience and the pure joy of finishing reports in about one-third the previous time, there is no turning back. For instance, those who compose directly on a typewriter or processor may type between forty and eighty words a minute. The writer struggling with longhand can usually write only 20 words a minute. With a little practice, you can dictate between 100 and 140 words a minute.

Whether you type or write, your mind often races ahead of your fingers. Many of the ideas and phrases you compose in your mind can be lost. The arithmetic is simple; the logic is undeniable. Portable dictation equipment enables you to tackle all the things that you've wanted to write, but never found the time for—updated bios, concept papers, article, outlines, and so forth.

Are you still unconvinced? Then try the following test. Time how long it takes you to write these sentences in longhand:

All else being equal, a portable dictation equipment user has greater career potential than those who don't indulge. Starting tomorrow, why not try some models?

Could you finish in under one minute? If you did finish in under a minute, is it legible? The above sentences contain only twenty-five words. Even if you dictate the sentence, with several pauses, you will still complete it in about twenty-five seconds. Proficient users can finish in under fifteen seconds.

Dictation can be used for almost *all* of your writing needs, from lengthy reports and letters to memos and notes to yourself. Nearly anything that takes more than five minutes to write can be done more easily dictated.

DO YOU NEED TO SEE IT?

Despite the obvious efficiency of dictating, many business executives and supervisors don't use dictation equipment and offer this rationale: "I like to see what I'm writing in progress." A visual review is helpful, but it is *not* necessary. Remember that a good outline is a prerequisite to effective writing—whether writing longhand or using other methods.

When dictating with a good outline, key words can readily be expanded into sentences and paragraphs. The pause feature on all portable dictation equipment allows you easily to start and stop to gather thoughts and to articulate complete sentences and paragraphs. Moreover, portable dictation equipment offers recall and playback features that allow you to monitor the recording as it progresses. Voice recognition software offers a variety of commands for making corrections and revisions.

With a good outline, the need to review what has been dictated diminishes in direct proportion to use of the equipment. It takes only two to four hours to become proficient.

Voice recognition software is available with ever-expanding capabilities. You can see your words appear on your PC screen, right after you dictate them. I want you to consider, however, that this is not necessarily a productivity enhancer! The need for visual review is overhyped. If you write longhand or via word processor, the desire for visual review increases due to the relatively slow progression. The human brain works faster—much faster. In other words, writing longhand or monitoring a screen reinforces the need for visual review. But dictating in 20- to 30-second blocks what may have previously required two to five minutes to write negates the need for visual review.

DICTAPHOBIA

Jefferson D. Bates, author of *Dictating Effectively: A Time Saving Manual*, points out that another big obstacle many people need to overcome before using dictation equipment regularly is "dictaphobia." To overcome dictaphobia, he says, "Recognize that putting words on tape or capturing them on voice recognition software is as easy as talking to a spouse, neighbor or office associate." He recommends the following steps in overcoming the fear of speaking into a dictaphone:

- Pick a subject you know well.
- Jot down a few ideas on the subject in outline form.
- Study the words for a few moments while the ideas sink in.
- Pick up the cassette recorder or don the headset that comes with your voice recognition software, close your eyes, and take several deep breaths (This helps put you in a creative state of mind).
- Imagine you're talking to a close friend or associate, anyone you feel comfortable with and trust. Picture that person in your mind.
- Start talking. If you still have hangups about getting started, take something you have handwritten earlier and start reading it aloud.

There's yet another advantage to dictating. Once you become accustomed to the process, it can encourage unmatched creativity in your writing. The speed and freedom dictation offers makes it much easier to capture fleeting ideas—and that's sure to pay off in concrete benefits to your career.

CHAPTER 14

MAINTAINING A LIST OF INTERNAL ACHIEVEMENTS

People who are really goal conscious don't spin their wheels. Their purpose is not to look and feel busy, but to achieve.
—Edwin C. Bliss

IF YOU'RE INTERESTED IN ACHIEVING MORE and using your achievements for career marketing, start by recognizing the achievements you've made—and then build from there. Your achievements are probably more substantial than you think. Most of us are so accustomed to what we do and what is expected of us on a daily basis that we don't think of our activities as real achievements. We're surprised when someone else is impressed with something we've done that seems rather ordinary to us.

Your prior achievements, when recalled and viewed properly, can encourage you to strive for future ones, so stay continually aware of them. Shrugging them off with modesty or forgetting about them can make it unnecessarily difficult to add more achievements to your repertoire.

I FEEL THE NEED, THE NEED TO ACHIEVE

While at Harvard University, David C. McClelland Ph.D., now at Boston University, identified three major factors that motivate people to varying degrees: the achievement motive, the affiliation motive, and the power motive. Most people have one of these as their dominant motive, while some individuals are high in all three. Since you decided to read this book, it's safe to say that you likely have a fairly high desire for achievement.

Professor McClelland determined these characteristics about people who are primarily motivated by achievements. See if any of the following matches up with you:

- They want to accomplish something significant.
- They like to set their own goals.
- They are eager to be their own boss; they do not like having people tell them what to do.
- They gravitate toward sales, marketing management, and independent businesses.
- They tend to be loners.
- They do not readily seek advice or help, but are willing to listen to experts.
- They tend to have low sensitivity toward others.
- They are not skilled in human relations.
- They are self-motivated.
- They want full responsibility for attaining their goals.
- They are always figuring the angles and taking calculated risks.
- They prefer to select moderate goals for themselves.
- They want immediate feedback on how well they are progressing toward their goals—such as sales, bonuses, or other concrete measures.
- They are not motivated to work harder by monetary incentives, but they do want to be paid well.
- They come mainly from middle-class families that set attainable goals and are supportive of their children.

The achievement-motivated individual, then, is quite different from the affiliation-motivated person, who is inspired by close interactions with others and good personal relationships. Likewise, the achievement-motivated individual differs from those who are motivated by power—striving for the status and authority that come with getting to the top.

McClelland believes that people can be taught the achievement motive. As they acquire strength in this area (although the other two areas of motivation probably will not be completely absent), they tend to become more self-confident, more enthusiastic about what they might be able to accomplish through their work, and more willing to take carefully calculated risks.

So, being motivated to achieve is good—especially in stimulating challenges and enthusiasm at work. People with low or no achievement motivation may find their work and their lives empty of vitality and vigor.

MAKING A LIST, CHECKING IT TWICE

I discovered that one of the best ways to keep myself in perspective about my achievements is keeping an Internal Achievements List. I developed this list to help me "consult" myself—to readily see gaps and problems, as well as successes.

I keep the list in chronological order, divided by month, over the span of a year. At the end of a year, I can see what I have (and haven't) achieved. You might be surprised at how much you do achieve in one year, and writing it down helps you to keep track. I restrict my list to those activities, awards, and milestones that signify that I've accomplished something. Whatever is an achievement for you—whether or not that achievement is recognized by others—goes on your list. For instance, you might regard finishing a project three days ahead of deadline as much an achievement as getting an award for the same project.

Here's an example—part of my Internal Achievements List for my last year as a full-time employee before becoming my own boss (many years ago!).

January: Appeared as one of eighteen presenters at the National Capital Speakers Association's first annual Speakers Showcase for area association, corporate, and government meeting planners and executives. Elected to the Board of Directors of National Capital Speakers Association and became chapter secretary.

February: Made an appearance on Warner Amex Cable TV Station Channel 8 in Reston, Virginia, as guest on Association Focus, which concentrated on how job seekers can use professional and trade associations to greatly enhance the job search process.

March: Selected as the Media Advocate of the Year for the District of Columbia by the U.S. Small Business Administration, winning it for the second consecutive year.

April: Cited by the American Institute of Management as an Executive of Distinction in the field of management along with Jack Kemp and Irving Black, CEO of duPont.

May: Interviewed for feature article by the *Christian Science Monitor* on streamlining your life through setting goals and personal time management.

As you can see, my Internal Achievements List reads like a note to myself—which it is. I don't attach it to biographical materials when I make speeches or write articles. However, even though I use it internally, it has wide-ranging spin-off benefits. For example, after I made up the first list, I began developing news releases about my monthly achievements, something I probably couldn't have done off the top of my head. Those news releases, in turn, helped my visibility.

The Internal Achievements List gets you moving and keeps you on target. Here are some of the major benefits of keeping, and frequently reviewing, such a list:

Measuring Your Progress—Seeing your achievements all in one place, in chronological order, helps you determine whether you are making the kind of professional and personal progress you want to make. You can readily see if what you've achieved is supportive of your goals; some achievements might simply take up time and energy without moving you toward those goals.

Commanding Attention—If you already have a clear picture of your accomplishments, you're way ahead in terms of letting your boss know why you merit that raise or promotion. It also helps an interviewer to know why you are the one to hire. You can promote yourself well when you know yourself well.

A Boost for Everything Else—Your internal list can be a boon when it's time to draft a resume, a biography, or other materials about yourself. The process of putting your abilities and history in writing is streamlined when you've already written out some of the most important factors.

Projecting Your Success—Once you've mastered the process of putting your achievements in writing, it makes sense that projecting your achievements into the future will also support your progress. The achievements that go into this log are the ones you realistically can accomplish, again arranged chronologically by month. Many of these can be drawn from your list of career goals.

Be realistic in determining your likely achievements a year into the future. Don't list everything you'd like to accomplish; stick to those items that you have a *reasonable* chance of accomplishing. You don't have to hedge your bets, however, by developing a short list that only includes the safe items and none of the achievements you'd have to strive to complete.

Your projected list, when properly compiled, acts as an incentive to spur you on and keep you on track, or remind you when you've taken a detour. If it's too optimistic, it will be discouraging and you'll shelve it. If it's not optimistic enough, the possibilities won't stimulate you.

Following is an example of a Projected Internal Achievements List:

January: Will complete and submit an article for publication. Will devise new secretary support system.

February: Will serve on at least one panel for the XYZ Society annual meeting. Will submit my name for one ongoing task force.

March: Will gather information for an article while on business trip to Portugal. Will vastly upgrade our division's website.

April: Will take out a summer membership in the local racquet and golf club and begin to network with business associates there.

May: Will complete application for national professional certification. Will speak to a student group touring Denver.

June: Will develop plan to split my department in two, with me as head of one of the new departments. Will gather documentation to support this change from inside and outside the company.

July: Will submit proposal to my boss and other top officials. Aim to receive my best-yet annual job evaluation, along with a 12 percent raise.

August: Will speak for our branch at the company's annual sales meeting in Newport.

September: Will receive my professional certification, as well as positive feedback about the proposal to split the department in two. Will be host on a weekly online forum.

October: Will volunteer for a tour of duty as orientation director for new employees in the department. Will begin conducting one or two orientation sessions a month.

November: Will submit, on request, further information on the plan to split the department. Will celebrate my fifth anniversary with the organization.

December: Will submit two newsletter articles on the profession to a national association. Will revise our 3,600-entry database.

This projected list is a "living" document that requires continual revision as achievements occur. All the while, maintain keen focus on what will propel both you and your organization forward!

PART V

YOUR WORLD TICKET: PROFESSIONAL EXPOSURE

CHAPTER 15

SPEAKERS ARE LEADERS

The most effective way to ensure the value of the future is to confront the present courageously and constructively.

—Rollo May

THIS CHAPTER COVERS THE TWO MAIN AREAS of concern for anyone who wishes to enter the world of public speaking: what to talk about and how to get invited to speak.

Here's a simple fact about career marketing: professionals who speak well in public are more likely to be promoted than those who don't. Also, public speaking can provide you with many new business contacts and possible additional income.

All About Your Speech

Have you ever had an experience that was so unusual or interesting that you had to share it? That's the best place to start. Another starting point is developing expertise in that subject area. If you can accept the challenge of communicating abstract ideas through practical examples, you may be a good candidate for public speaking.

I can vividly recall the first time I ever spoke to a group professionally. I was speaking to about seventy-five entrepreneurs at the Hartford District Office of the Small Business Administration. At the time I was working for a management consulting firm that provided marketing and management assistance to small- to medium-sized businesses. One of our marketing activities to gain exposure for the firm was to serve as seminar leaders at SBA-sponsored workshops.

Although I had only been with the company six months, this Tuesday in May was to be my public speaking initiation. The presentation was to last thirty minutes. I was prepared and qualified, having offered the same type of advice to individuals on a one-to-one basis for two years.

When I got in front of the group, everything changed. The words were coming out and what I was saying had impact, but my stomach was doing somersaults. By the end of the session, a feather could have knocked me over; I was lightheaded, dizzy, exhilarated, and glad I was finished.

In the months that followed, the presentation became easier and easier to give. I think it was after the sixth time that the butterflies left and my feet were firmly planted. And a funny thing happened by the next year—I actually started looking forward to speaking before groups. All of the things that I had read about the nervous energy that never dissipates didn't seem to apply. In succeeding years, I was better prepared to communicate on the job, impressed bosses and coworkers with the names of groups I had spoken to, and acquired confidence that spilled over into other areas of my career.

You may have never considered speaking in public, yet becoming a good public speaker can help you to advance your career rapidly. Not only will you be perceived as bold and dynamic, but you'll also gain visibility and new business contacts or clients.

SPEAKING PREPARATION

"The surest way to turn off an audience is to read a speech," says Maggie Bedrosian, author of *Speak Like a Pro*. People came to hear you speak, not to hear you read. Your first step in preparing your speech is to focus on exactly what you want your speech to convey to the group. Try describing the impact you want in one sentence. Then tackle two or three ideas at most. It's more effective to illustrate a few ideas in depth than to touch on a wide variety of topics. Examples and anecdotes will help your audience remember the main points.

You can't go wrong following the old adage, "Tell 'em what you're going to tell 'em, tell 'em, and then tell 'em what you told 'em."

A few initial tips on the three parts of a speech—the opening, the middle, and the closing. A strong opening is vital to holding your audience's attention. If figures can document your point, use them. Be careful, however—don't overwhelm your audience with figures throughout the speech. Members of the group will be disinterested if they hear too many numbers after the first third or so of your presentation.

The body or middle of your speech is the meat of it. Here you strive to be compelling, alluring, insightful, and watchable. If you're going to lose members of the audience, here is where it's most likely. Some may nod off, others may daydream. Some may give you stares of false attention. I always take the attitude that it's not my audience's responsibility to stay interested in what I'm saying— it's my responsibility to get them and keep them interested!

Your conclusion is as important, if not more so, than anything in your speech. Make it dynamic, drawing together the points you have made in your speech with a strong example or anecdote.

PLOT IT OUT

After you've decided on your opening and closing, outline the important parts of the body of your speech.

When outlining, use key words to remind yourself of the key points. Writing out whole sentences is unnecessary and burdensome.

Practice your speech using the outline, written on notecards or with any other method that's comfortable for you. Your speech will be different each time you practice it. Don't worry about that. It will be different for each audience as well. The secret of becoming a good public speaker is the ability to turn a speech, even to a huge audience, into a two-way conversation. You modify your speech based on the energy level, intellectual understanding, enthusiasm, and many other characteristics of the audience.

Use the active voice at all times during your speech. If you use an unfamiliar or technical word that your audience may not know, rephrase it or define it in the next sentence without being condescending.

DELIVER WITH STYLE

Believe in your message and its importance to your audience. Lou Hampton, a professional speaker and executive speech coach who has trained members of Congress, says, "Become interested enough in your audience that your prime concern is how to get your message from you to them. When you think more about how you're going to put your message across and less about what people will think of you, you'll end up a better communicator. Allow yourself to release your energy in a positive way."

Maggie Bedrosian advocates applying the "iceberg formula" to keep an audience interested. She describes great speakers as those who have a broad-based knowledge of their field but exhibit power by suggesting much greater knowledge.

"Such a speaker leaves most audiences hungering for more, as it should be. A 'hungry' audience will be moved to action. They are more inclined to explore further to seek results. A 'satisfied' group, on the other hand, may walk away thinking, 'Oh, that's nice. I wonder what's on the late show tonight,'" relates Bedrosian. The point of your presentation is "to stimulate the group into action, not satisfy them into complacency."

A FEW (NOT SO MINOR) DETAILS

If you must use notecards, place them on the lectern or table from which you'll be speaking. However, move away from the lectern whenever possible. A speaker who moves a little seems more dynamic and involved, even if he or she uses the same words as a speaker frozen behind the lectern. Furniture separates you from your audience. Once you get comfortable, step out from behind it; eventually, you'll wonder why you ever needed it in the first place.

Your intonation is also important. Vary your pitch, tone, and speech according to the emphasis on your content. Tape one or two of your practice sessions to help you judge how you sound to an audience (see Figures 15-1 and 15-2 for speaking checklists).

FIGURE 15-1, JUDGING THE FINE POINTS

The following items are important in speeches:

- **Content** Ideas, reception, description, logic.
- **Speech Development** Organization, thought, continuity.
- **Speech Structure** Opening, body, closing.
- **Language** Pronunciation, grammar, appropriateness.
- **Manner** Assurance, directness, enthusiasm.
- **Voice** Volume, pitch, use, flexibility.
- **Physical** Gestures, movement, poise.

Figure 15-2, Tips for Humorous Speeches

Here are important components for humorous speeches:

- **Speech Development** Structure, opening, body, closing organization, support material.
- **Effectiveness** Excitement, created suspense, the unexpected twist, surprise, connection of humorous events, achievement of purpose.
- **Image** Appearance, body language.
- **Originality** Ideas, novelty of thought and material.
- **Audience Response** Attentiveness, laughter, interest, reception.

Many speech coaches will tell you that most people speak several tones too high. The reason—they don't hear their voices as others do. "The sound reaches them through the head rather than through vibration in the air, distorting the tone," says one coach. The antidote is to use lots of jaw and lip movement. "This will improve tone and make you look more animated. It will also slow your delivery, which gives you more time to think of what you want to say."

Lou Hampton recalls a corporate president with whom he worked. "During the training session, he did a run-through of a presentation he was going to give at the annual stockholders meeting. It had been an extremely good year for the company. Sales and profits had increased dramatically. When we replayed the videotape, I turned to him and said, 'Well, Tom, what do you think?' He said, 'Based on how I look and my tone of voice, they'll think we had a rotten year!'"

Allow yourself to be expressive and natural in illustrating your points. "Most of us," says Hampton, "gesture when we're speaking one-on-one, but clam up in front of a group." Do what you would do in conversation.

Occasionally, someone will insist that he or she simply doesn't gesture. "One corporate executive we worked with was adamant that he did not gesture. The training session was interrupted by a call from his corporate headquarters. A division vice president needed an answer on some national advertising being planned," recalls Hampton.

"We stopped the training session for half an hour while the client and his top assistants held a meeting. While discussing the situation, our client was leaning back in his chair, gesturing with large, expressive, smooth movements. Gesturing was natural for him, as it is for most people. I carefully observed each of his gestures and then immediately conveyed what I had seen. We reconvened our training session, and his reluctance to gesture had vanished."

MAKING EYE CONTACT

Closely related to the ability to convey your energy is the quiet skill of prolonged eye contact. This involves maintaining eye contact with an individual for three, four, or five seconds, or until you have completed a thought. Most speakers look at people momentarily before moving to someone else, scanning the audience rather than establishing specific eye contact. Don't let yourself slide into this habit.

It's important to establish eye contact because it helps to reduce your tension. Also, by focusing on one person at a time you remind yourself that you're in a conversation. Even with a room of 500 people, everyone you speak to is interpreting you individually and will respond to you individually. If you look at somebody for three to five seconds, you have time to actually to see that individual. That will enable you to read the whole audience. You'll know, or sense, how they're responding.

HANDOUTS

We're not talking about food for the homeless here. It's a good idea to distribute information with or directly following your presentation. If you distribute article reprints or other written material at the speaking engagement, you'll at least ensure that your audience leaves with your correct name and address. It also gives them something tangible with which to remember you.

Frequently, I also use an audience pre-speech questionnaire, distributed at the outset, to quickly gauge what listeners came to hear (see the example in Figure 15-3).

FIGURE 15-3, AUDIENCE QUESTIONNAIRE

Jeff Davidson, CMC ▪ 2417 Honeysuckle Road ▪ Chapel Hill, NC 27514 ▪ (919)932-1996

DATE _____ NAME OF WORKSHOP _____

NAME _____

MAILING ADDRESS _____

_____

TITLE AT WORK _____

ORGANIZATION/AGENCY_____

_____

_____

PHONE _____(w)_____(h)

FAX _____ E-MAIL_____

In your wildest dreams, what will you learn in this workshop?

What is the *minimum* you want to learn in order to leave feeling satisfied?

PUBLIC SPEAKING IN PERSPECTIVE

Speeches or presentations don't necessarily bring instant results. One professional consulting firm reports that it has received telephone calls from targets who heard a member of the firm speak several years previously.

While you may make speeches with the idea of advancing your career or gaining new business, never turn your speech into a direct attempt to self-promote or to make a sales pitch or sales presentation. Speak on a topic of interest and do your best; anything else is a turnoff and can backfire.

Your decision on whether to seek speaking engagements as a personal promotional tool hinges on two things: 1) your ability to be interesting, and 2) having something worthwhile to say to a group composed of targets of opportunity or influence. If you have never spoken before a group, you have a unique experience in store. Everyone is nervous at first, but after a while you may find public speaking to be quite exhilarating.

Getting the Word Out

A couple of years before leaving the world of working for others, I spoke to more than forty local groups while still employed full time. My strategy for getting invited was simple. Each week I opened my local paper to the section on professional meetings. I called all the meeting planners listed and suggested that their members might benefit from my presentation. Often I did this for no fee. In turn, I developed my speaking skills, gained exposure within the professional community, and converted tape transcripts into articles for publication. Soon, I developed a brief flyer, which accelerated the number of requests (see Figure 15-4 for that early layout example, modified with current information).

FIGURE 15-4, PUBLIC SPEAKING FLYER

JEFF DAVIDSON, CMC

Can help you to:

- Manage the pace with grace
- Handle information overload
- Have more, do less
- Get ahead and stay ahead
- Have more breathing space

Credentials	Certified Management Consultant (CMC) consulting designation. 18 years—280 consulting clients, 525 speaking engagements. Marketing, MBA degrees.
Writing	25 Books, 3,250 articles published. Credits: *Washington Post, Executive Review, Toastmaster, Leaders, Executive Excellence, Selling Power.* Award winner: Small Business Administration "Media Advocate of the Year," "Outstanding Young Men in America," and 21 book club selections
Affiliation:	Institute of Management Consultants National Speakers Association Carolina Speakers Association Association Executive of North Carolina

FIGURE 15-4, CONTINUED

Speaking Engagements:	IBM, Executone, American Online, Re/Max Swissotel, National Association of Realtors NationsBank, Dollar Rent-a-Car, IMC-YMCA American Express, Westinghouse, I.R.S.
Frequently Requested Topics:	▪ Relaxing at High Speed ▪ Managing Multiple Priorities ▪ Managing Information Overload ▪ Managing the Pace with Grace ▪ How to Have More Breathing Space
Address:	2417 Honeysuckle Road, Suite 2A Chapel Hill, NC 27514-6819 Ph 919-932-1996 Fax 919-932-9982 Jeffspeaks@BreathingSpace.com http://www.BreathingSpace.com

Typing a one-page letter explaining a little about your background will help to spread the word on your availability. Also include a short description of your (three to five) topics. You might say something like, "My most frequently requested topics are: starting your own business, record-keeping aspects of managing your own business, standing up to the IRS, developing a management style, and common mistakes of successful business professionals." List only those topics on which you can speak quite comfortably and about which you could answer questions.

Distribute your letter to perhaps as many as fifty groups in your local area. As a result of this one mailing, you could generate two to five speaking engagements. For this or any other mailing, it's wise to send a second letter or to have someone on your staff make a follow-up telephone call.

TO WHOM TO SPEAK

Many local groups (civic and charitable associations) actively seek speakers. Yet the program directors of these groups often have to scramble to find an interesting one. Check your local newspaper as I did for the calendar of events that will list seminars offered by organization. You'll probably be surprised by the number and variety of meetings in even the smallest community. Also, identify any adult education programs. I polished my presentations for eight years with a Washington, D.C., outfit, offering as many as eight different seminars.

The best way to be invited to speak to a local organization is by being a member of that group. But whether you're a member or not, be sure to contact meeting planners at least twice. You can call first, then mail your materials and make a follow-up telephone call to each organization receiving your letter. This reinforces your desire to speak before that group. Or, you can simply mail first and then call. Personally, I find the first sequence to be more effective. Use e-mail only after you've established a relationship.

THE LOOMING EVENT

When some requests arrive, you'll need some additional information before preparing your speech. To increase the effectiveness of your presentation, find out the size of the room, the setup (rows of seats, small tables, some other arrangement?), the expected attendance, the program length, the names and subject areas of any other speakers, the available sound system and audiovisual equipment, and the usual temperature and lighting in the speaking room (see the checklist in Figure 15-5).

FIGURE 15-5, SPEAKING ENGAGEMENT CHECKLIST

Meeting place

Size of room _____

Setup _____ Seating capacity _____

Sound system _____ Audiovisuals _____

Temperature/ventilation _____

Surrounding rooms_____

Comments _____

_____

Audience Profile

Ages _____ Male/Female ratio_____ Educational level_____

Professional experience (years) _____ Number of attendees _____

Goals _____

Obstacles _____

Job description _____

Comments _____

_____

Ask whether you're responsible for operating audiovisual equipment. If you're not convinced of the importance of such details, try to recall the message of the last speaker you heard while sitting in a 90-degree room!

SPEAKING ORGANIZATIONS

To further your speaking capabilities, there are two organizations you may consider joining.

The National Speakers Association is the professional association for public speakers. As a member, you receive inside information and the opportunity to network with and learn from some of the top professional speakers in the world today. This is a friendly group, and practically everyone is willing to share information with you.

The National Speakers Association has local chapters across the country. As one speaker put it, "Here's where the action is year round. Ongoing programs to develop your skills, networking with local, friendly, professional speakers and business people like yourself, and new opportunities—all are yours at the local chapter level." NSA has more than thirty chapters. Your local chapter will welcome your interest. For more details, contact the association at:

National Speakers Association
1500 S. Priest Avenue
Tempe, AZ 88014
602-968-2552

Also, contact your local Toastmasters chapter. Toastmasters is a worldwide organization with thousands of local chapters, which provides training in speaking skills. While NSA and Toastmasters often approach different aspects of speaking, their programs are complementary. Many aspiring speakers belong to both. In NSA you discover the aspects of speaking professionally. Toastmasters is more oriented toward nuts-and-bolts speaking skills with feedback and evaluation.

Toastmasters chapters often exist within large corporations for their employees; usually chapters are independent and open to the public. For a chapter near you, contact:

Toastmasters International
P.O. Box 9052
Mission Viejo, CA 92690
949-858-8255

CHAPTER 16

THE ART OF
NETWORKING

Nature takes away any faculty that is not used.
—William R. Inge

BOTH NETWORKING AND JOINING CERTAIN GROUPS and organizations can be important factors in your career marketing. Networking—making potentially useful contacts and building relationships with individuals, groups, and organizations—has been, and remains, an integral factor in business. Concurrently, there's a true business magic in joining professional, civic, charitable, and social groups that's difficult to describe. Let's consider both of these career-marketing strategies.

Networking

Many people believe that networking means interacting with everyone with whom they come in contact. Not so! Whatever your field or profession, there are probably only ten to twenty people that you need to know to accelerate your career.

Who are these key people? I'll bet you already know who they are. In my case they are key meeting planners, publishers, agents, and media people. For you, the answer may be colleagues, editors of industry publications, the directors of professional associations in your industry, leading business people from your community, a career counselor, a mentor, or perhaps someone in another department of your organization.

Let's face it—a large part of your career success is based on other people. Certainly you have to be good at what you do. However, as a total "package" you want to continually be improving, communicative, and forward-thinking. The business "woods" are full of highly competent, well-trained, dedicated professionals who do their jobs but seldom advance. They lack that well-rounded "human" component that their bosses need to see for promotion.

Networking (and also joining associations) is a process worth maintaining whether you're looking for a new job or seeking to advance within your company. Rest assured that networking is an ongoing part of most successful professionals' lives. Networking serves many functions, including job searches, accelerated career climb, and professional fellowship. Those with an ingrained sense of career marketing recognize that what you learn and the contacts you make outside the job help advance your career. Why? Because at the same time that you're constantly embracing new ideas, new people, new thoughts, and new ways of looking at things, you're increasing *your* exposure.

NETWORKING MEANS ACTION

Networking can be as simple as a telephone call to someone you worked with years ago, or as complex as analyzing several trade associations most beneficial to your career advancement. It's a continual process of sharing, passing along, and receiving information that can help with your personal or business advancement.

Talk to everyone you can at professional meetings and gatherings. Later, make notes on the back of each card of conversation points that will help the person remember you. For example, if you decide to follow up, say, "Hi, we met at the Cosmos Club and talked about foreign hi-tech markets." Depending on the number of cards you collect, go through them weekly or monthly to weed them out. Questions to ponder when deciding which contacts to follow up include:

- Do I like this person?
- Did I feel challenged, excited by our conversation?
- Does this person have high energy?
- Does this person have knowledge I need or want?
- Does this person have contacts in my field?
- Could this person help advance my career at some time?
- Could I help this person with his or her career?

Be selective. You can't be effective with an extended network.

THE RIGHT STUFF

An effective network is composed of two different kinds of supporters: maintainers and propellers. Maintainers are those who help you get your job done competently and effectively; propellers push you into new areas to promote your advancement.

Figure 16-1 can help you examine your network and find where to make improvements. First, write in the names of people in your network who fit into each category in the left column. Next, in the right column, fill in the names, where possible, of people whom you *would like* as part of your network in those categories. Where you don't know a specific person, identify someone who can direct you in your search.

FIGURE 16-1, EFFECTIVE NETWORKING

MAINTAINERS

	Present	Future
KEYSTONES—People who form the core of your network and are fundamental to getting your job done (e.g., an administrative assistant).	_____ _____	_____ _____
EXPERTS—Although these people do not propel your career, they are people in your field whom you respect and value as professional contacts and would recommend to others; those on whose professional competence you would stake your reputation.	_____ _____ _____ _____	_____ _____ _____ _____
TANGENTIAL HELPERS—People in related fields who help you get your job done (e.g., a writer needs an editor, publisher, and a graphic designer).	_____ _____ _____ _____	_____ _____ _____ _____

PROPELLERS

	Present	Future
MENTORS—People who guide your career, provide opportunity and access, and teach you the ropes (see Chapter 4).	_____ _____	_____ _____
ROLE MODELS—People whose professional behavior stimulates ideas for your future. They have achieved what you aspire to; they are examples to emulate.	_____ _____	_____ _____
HUBS—Those who refer you to additional sources of information and people. They suggest helpful connections.	_____ _____	_____ _____
CHALLENGERS—People who cause you to look at your own direction, and force you to face some important questions about your life.	_____ _____	_____ _____
PROMOTERS/RECOMMENDERS—People who advise you of opportunities and encourage your visibility.	_____ _____	_____ _____

GETTING FORMAL ABOUT NETWORKING

Formal networking is more direct than the rather informal networking discussed so far. A major purpose of trade associations and professional groups is information-sharing and networking. It's useful to join a professional organization, not only in your current field but in fields that interest you as well.

The following list offers examples of potential networking goals:

- Meet one new person in my profession each week.
- Attend two major professional conventions this year.
- Write to five leading authors by the end of the month.
- Join two new local organizations comprised of community business leaders.
- Call all 168 people on my contact management software in the next three months (an average of only two per day).
- Obtain a directory of professionals in my field and become familiar with those who live within the state.
- Attend three mixers as a potential member of a group, such as the Chamber of Commerce, Board of Trade, or United Way.

Networking can be useful if you remember to keep it focused, weeding out contacts periodically and recognizing that it's a continual process of sharing information and favors.

In as little as six months, you may find that you have completely revitalized your address book. People open doors for you, and by undertaking a focused approach to networking, you can make contact with the right "keys."

Joining with a Purpose

During my fifth year in the working world, I joined Washington Independent Writers because I like to write. The number of articles that I was writing after work and on weekends led me to believe that someday I might have a future in writing. Two years later, I joined another professional group specifically to increase my exposure and professionalism. Jefferson D. Bates, the aforementioned author of *Dictating Effectively*, invited me to a monthly meeting of National Capital Speakers Association, the Washington, D.C., chapter of the National Speakers Association.

At my first meeting I experienced a personal revelation. Here I met people who were highly enthusiastic and who had important messages to offer. Some of them delivered seminars and training sessions locally; others spoke across the country on a full-time basis, and for healthy fees. As the youngest person at this meeting, you can imagine what solid, eye-opening contacts awaited me.

Today I still belong to that association and my membership has paid off greatly. I have since joined the Association Executives of North Carolina, Carolina Speakers Association, and the Institute of Management Consultants.

DO YOU BELIEVE IN MAGIC?

The magic that unfolds when you join professional, civic, charitable, and social groups is hard to describe. When you join these types of organizations, you're rubbing elbows with the winners in society. If you traveled across the country, stopping in any city, you could readily find the most prosperous people in the community by simply heading toward the hotels, restaurants, or convention centers—any place where there are meeting rooms. Read the marquee to see who is in attendance, go up to the registration table, and tell them you would like to learn more about that group.

You might ask what *specific* benefits I received as a result of my various memberships. My membership in Washington Independent Writers enabled me to meet other authors throughout the region. Many offered valuable tips on getting an agent, getting an advance for books, preparing manuscript proposals, and assisting the publisher with marketing once the book is published.

As a result of joining the National Capital Speakers Association, I raised my speaking fee in that year alone from $185 to $480. I subsequently raised it again to $750, then to $1,200, $1,800, $2,250, $3,500, $5,000, $6,000, and now even more than that. When I first joined National Capital Speakers, I didn't believe anybody in the world could get more than a couple of hundred dollars for a speaking engagement. But befriending and networking with people who regularly did was all the evidence I needed. These, of course, are only two examples of specific benefits I received from networking.

I was fortunate to be among the youngest in all the groups that I joined. It's rewarding to be with your own age group, but for accelerated career advancement, I recommend meeting with those who are five, ten, and even many more years your senior.

VOLUNTEER FOR SUCCESS

Earning a position of leadership in a high visibility organization is an excellent way to be of service and, as a by-product, enhance your career potential. Smart business leaders know that giving their time freely is an excellent way to be of service to the community and to help develop a solid professional and personal reputation. And, you get the supreme opportunity to interact with key community and business leaders to work jointly on solving local problems.

While you're gaining exposure, others in the group will assume that you are fully competent in your profession and a rising star in the community, another key benefit of joining such an organization.

By volunteering your services and assisting civic and charitable organizations, targets of opportunity—those who may provide your next job—come to know you as a person they can feel comfortable discussing business opportunities and problems with. Your organizational skills will become evident in the course of your association with a group. Do you volunteer for committee activities? Do you deliver what you promise? Can you handle leadership within the group? If so, you could get the attention of someone who could advance your career.

JOINING SELECTIVELY

Any local group tends to be run by small cliques. The lead time necessary to break into these subgroups and begin accruing benefits from the organization can range anywhere from six to eighteen months. Many professionals don't stand their ground. They drop out and never realize that the benefits of being known and accepted in the group were "just around the corner."

Despite the advantages, joining professional and civic groups can be a drain on your time and energy if you are not selective. Evaluate your memberships in these groups to determine:

- If you're meeting and working with people who could help in your career advancement.
- If you're personally satisfied with the group's activities.
- If you like the people in the organization.
- If the long-term benefits will equal the energy and time you spend now.

Each community is somewhat different and the interplay of political, social, cultural, and religious spheres varies, so carefully consider what groups to join and why. Continually analyze local organizational contacts for relationships to develop, and pay particular attention to senior executives and entrepreneurs who may be expanding operations.

Balance this approach, however, with the realization that the only organizations you would want to join are those in which you have a genuine interest and desire to serve. Purely Machiavellian aims seldom pay off and can cause resentment among others in the organization.

ORGANIZATIONS FOR ALL OCCASIONS

The following list includes national as well as local organizations that are likely to have chapters in your area. Check your local telephone book for the address of any group that interests you and call for membership information.

FIGURE 16-2, GROUPS TO JOIN

Active Corps of Executives
American Business Women's
  Association
American Cancer Society
American Heart Association
American Marketing
  Association
Boys' Club Boosters
Chamber of Commerce
Civitans
Democratic party
Easter Seal Campaign
Elks
Explorers
Garden clubs
Goodwill Industries
Heart Fund
Historical Society
Independent party
International Association of
  Business Communicators
Jaycees
Kiwanis
League of Women Voters
Lions
March of Dimes

Masons
Moose
Multiple Sclerosis Society
National Association of
  Professional Saleswomen
National Association of Women
  Business Owners
Optimists Club
Parent-Teacher Association
Public Television
Republican party
Rotary Club
Sales Executives International
Salvation Army
Scouts of America
Sertomas
Society of Association
  Executives
Toastmasters
United Way
Urban League
Variety Club
VFW
YMCA
YWCA
Zoo Foundation

MAXIMIZE IT: COMMITTEES ARE THE KEY

The work of the organization is done in committees. They usually have specific tasks, meeting more often than the general membership and offering more of a chance for the camaraderie that is natural in small group work. A position such as activities chair gives you high visibility and virtually unlimited access to key members. The membership committee or social committee can also offer a high visibility position.

Caution: Although it's important to volunteer for committee activities, take on only what you can realistically accomplish. Nothing turns off a group more quickly than unkept promises. Excuses, no matter how good they seem to you, will fall flat to a group that has counted on your work.

If Joe Smith tells you he's interested in your ideas on creative financing that you discussed over coffee at the last United Way meeting, follow up quickly and professionally. Most people don't follow up. You'll quickly find out whether Joe was serious or not, but either way, he'll remember your initiative.

QUIET COMMITMENT

Don't wave your membership in a civic organization like a flag. Quiet, subtle references will ensure that your commitment to the group gets noticed. Every once in a while, do something on behalf of the organization without mentioning it.

Appendix A offers some professional organizations to consider joining. With every group you join, constantly monitor and analyze your memberships to make sure you are getting a good return for the time invested. Remember to join only groups in which you have a genuine interest and desire to serve.

Finally, for the most effective career marketing, meet and *be remembered by* your network.

CHAPTER 17

BREAKING INTO PRINT

*Whatever you want to do, do it now. There
are only so many tomorrows.*

—Michael Landon

YEARS AGO, AS AN EMPLOYEE OF A SMALL CONSULTING firm in Connecticut, I approached my boss during a slow period in the work week and asked what I could do to help the firm during this time. He suggested writing an article, an activity that would *never* have occurred to me, a B-student in English composition with no thought of writing.

After several false starts, I hit on a simple formula to help me through my first piece. The title of the article was "Ten Tips on Survival for Small Business." The concept was simple. I'd come up with ten different tips that would be the start of a paragraph or two. I would then add opening and closing paragraphs and that would be my whole article. The article was easy to write. As I later found, when you attach a number to your title, such as "Eight Ways to . . .," you finish the article with less struggle, even if you don't come up with eight ways (you might only reach six).

We mailed my manuscript out to a publication that sat on it for five months and then rejected it. We then mailed it to another magazine, *The New Englander*, which sat on it for four months. One day, without advance notice or word of any kind, a package arrived. It was thick. I opened it and found that my article, "Ten Tips on Survival for Small Business," had been published in the current issue of *The New Englander* magazine. As it turned out, it was the last article in the issue—the least of my concerns. The graphics and artwork that they had done were wonderful and the article made an attractive reprint. I was so excited to have my name in print that I probably photocopied that article 500 times and sent it to everyone I knew.

Although the magazine paid me nothing, the lesson I learned was priceless. Up until then I thought that only superstars and the privileged classes got their names in print. When I discovered portable dictation equipment a couple years later, I began dictating articles at the pace of about one a month, increasing within a year to one per week.

PUBLISHING PAYS OFF

It's important to have realistic expectations of what publishing can do for you. Publishing articles in newspapers and magazines can accelerate career marketing efforts and offer a sense of pride. Publishing probably won't put you on the best-seller list or get you on Jay Leno. However, all other things being equal, if you've had a couple of articles published, you're better positioned for advancement than a coworker who hasn't. Check out these benefits:

Positions you as an expert—Getting published means credentials for you in the article subject area. If a supervisor in an engineering firm, for example, writes an article on reinforcing bridge supports, a public notice has been made that he or she, and the firm, are experts in this area. Someone requiring a subcontractor on a bridge design project may call the writer's organization merely on the basis of the article.

Gain ever-wider acceptance—If you concentrate on one subject area, you're likely to gain ever-wider acceptance with magazines in your field, and you can keep up with new developments while increasing your visibility.

Makes for attractive reprints—You can create a favorable impression by supplying clients, coworkers, and peers with reprints of an article you've had published. Modesty aside, most authors are proud of their work and have no qualms about submitting reprints to friends, relatives, and associates. Most people are pleased and impressed to accept your reprint. Of course, use this technique discreetly to avoid seeming egotistical.

Supports career changes—You can include reprints of your article with resumes when applying for a new position and with raise requests at your present job.

Invites speaking invitations—An article can lead to an invitation to speak before a particular group. Every article can be made into a speech, and vice versa. Giving speeches will put you in touch with others interested in your subject area, who will in turn help broaden your web of connections. This circular exchange of information can prove highly beneficial.

Visibility for you and your organization—Always mention your organization in your bio when you write an article. For example, "Joe Smith is a manager of XYZ Corporation." Your article therefore will market both you and your organization. If possible, without stretching the content, you may want to mention your company's name in the body of the article (Use caution, however, with this technique. Some organizations are sensitive about publicity and would prefer *not* to be mentioned in connection with an employee's activities. Check out your organization's *unwritten* rules in this area before going ahead.)

The benefits of getting published will continue for a surprisingly long time. A friend of mine got a letter about an article he had published in a monthly trade magazine two-and-a-half years before. This isn't unusual. Your article will live on as long as there are libraries.

PUBLISHING MARKETS

The number of general, industrial, business, professional, and in-house publications has risen dramatically in recent years. First, try your own organization's in-house newsletter if you're in a large organization, or the in-house publications of companies in your field. Their personnel or human resources department will usually be responsible for the newsletter's publication, or will know who is.

You can obtain the name, address, telephone number, editorial content, fees paid, circulation, target audience, and submission requirements for more than 10,000 journals and magazines by checking one of the following directories in the reference section of your library:

Bacon's Magazine Directory
Bacon's Newspaper Directory
Working Press of the Nation
Writer's Market
Oxbridge Directory of Publications
Standard Periodicals Directory

What about getting published on the Internet via an online 'zine such as *Slate*, *Salon*, or *Fast Company*? Sure, these offer some status, but they still cannot compete with hard copy, circulated publications. Also, online articles don't make for reprints as attractive or prestigious as hard copy reprints.

To help you get started, the names and addresses of dozens of business, management, and career-related magazines and journals are listed in Appendix B.

CHOOSING A TOPIC

The best topics for articles are derived from successful work that you've already done. This includes reports, papers, summaries, guides, and exhibits that you've prepared, perhaps for work, which can be generalized and applied to a larger audience. Even if you've never written about a subject, you may have an article if you have special knowledge or insights.

Here are some ways to generate article topics and start getting published.

Clip articles that stimulate you—Every time you read the Sunday newspaper or a professional journal, save articles that strike your fancy. You might not even know how you'd use the article when you clip it. File all of the clippings by topic or subject area. Months later, review your clip file, and you'll find that what you've clipped serves as the catalyst for numerous article ideas. Freelance writers have successfully used the clip file technique for years.

To aid in your "clipping" efforts, write to Luce Press Clippings and ask for a free newspaper clipper. This is a small plastic device that helps you to deftly and neatly extract articles from newspapers and magazines. Contact:

Luce Press Clippings
42 S. Center Street
Mesa, AZ 85210-1397
800-528-8226

Think "how to"—Think of six, eight, or more ways to do something better. The market for "how to" articles is strong as more and more people thirst for "do-it-yourself" information. By putting a number into the title of your article, such as "7 Ways to Accomplish XYZ," you have a hook that will attract readers.

(Figure 17-1 shows 10 generic article topics, and Figure 17-2 shows how these topics were turned into potential articles.)

FIGURE 17-1, GENERIC ARTICLE TOPICS

How to _____

_____ Reasons Why _____

_____ Ways to Improve _____

_____ to Consider Before _____

_____ Pitfalls _____

New Developments _____

A _____ Approach to _____

The Art of _____

Overcoming Resistance to _____

Planning for Your _____

List your gripes—A list of gripes or discomforts in connection with your work can actually contain the seeds of articles. If something bothers you, it undoubtedly bothers others. Discuss the problem in broad terms and offer suggestions for redress. By recognizing the universality of a problem that you face, you'll be creating material for an excellent article.

Remember the memorable—An unforgettable staff member (or boss), a favorite professional experience, your biggest disappointment, or other memorable event can lead to some underlying lesson, something we can all use in our lives.

Focus on your potential readers—If you concentrate for a moment on who will be reading your article and what impact it will have on them, your writing will flow more smoothly. Think of the last time you wrote a letter to a friend or relative. Your writing task was on a one-to-one basis and your target audience was perfectly defined. Your words and ideas probably flowed freely. You can achieve the same effect when you precisely define the target group that will be reading your article. If it helps, write the name of your target group on the top of your outline, such as "peers," "project staff," or "executives earning over $180,000 per year."

AVOID STARTING FROM SCRATCH

Don't write an article from scratch. It's too much work! Possibly the best tip I can offer is to review all of the reports, proposals, papers, memos, outlines, and such that you've ever written and saved to determine their applicability as articles. As a management consultant, at the end of each engagement I had to write a client report. From those reports I was frequently able to pull out five- and six-page passages that could be generalized and applied to a larger audience.

I bet that if you've held on to your college papers, you might find one or two publishable articles from term papers and compositions that you turned in for a letter grade. You'll be amazed to find that editors of publications are often much easier to deal with than your professors were. Also, remember the larger articles sometimes make wonderful shorter articles.

FIGURE 17-2, POTENTIAL ARTICLES

- How to Ask for a Bigger Office
- Six Reasons Why Using a PC Will Decrease Your Efficiency
- Eight Ways to Improve Your Vocabulary
- Items to Consider Before Changing Jobs
- Four Pitfalls in Working for a Government Agency
- The Art of Closing the Sale
- New Developments in Laser Technology
- A New Approach to Group Decision-Making
- Overcoming Resistance to Reorganization
- Planning for Your Next Job Promotion

SPIN IT AROUND

If you've already written one article, producing spinoff articles is a marvelous technique for generating other articles. For example, I wrote an article entitled, "How to Build a Law Practice," following a consulting engagement I had with a Washington, D.C., law firm. The article essentially followed a "14 tips" format although I didn't use that title. I sent the article to *Case and Comment* in Rochester, New York, which accepted it for publication.

About a year later I was going through my files and came across the article. It dawned on me that with little time and effort I could convert that article to "How to Build a Medical Practice." In the previous year I'd worked with a couple of doctors and dentists and was now familiar with their terminology and the differences required to restructure my earlier article. I reworked "How to Build a Law Practice" fourteen times, including versions for dentists, real estate agents, insurance agents, accountants, graphic artists, consultants, and others.

If selecting an article topic is difficult for you or if you suffer from writer's block, consider those articles and those topics that lend themselves to spin-offs, and you'll find yourself doubling, tripling, and quadrupling your publishing efforts!

STOP READING, START WRITING

Most people agree that having an article published is a worthwhile endeavor. At speaking engagements, I frequently point out that if you stop reading the Sunday paper a few times every couple of months and devote that time to writing an article, in the course of the year you could have three or four articles written and, perhaps, published. By the end of three or four years, you might have between six and ten articles published. This would put you in the upper one percent of the population in terms of being in print.

Also, think of all the times that you read the Sunday newspaper and within three days forgot most of it. Analyze what the continual reading of the newspaper has done for your income, career, and life and you'll agree that you could skip reading the newspaper now and then, write an article, and enjoy the benefits of getting published.

UNBLOCKING WRITER'S BLOCK

Writer's block hangs heavy over the heads of many career marketers. If writer's block is a problem for you, the following suggestions may help you to get started:

Outline your ideas—Producing a one-page outline, or writing as little as ten key words on a page, can guide me through the preparation and completion of an article. Devote a block of time to simply preparing article outlines or chronological sequences that can later serve as a useful tool when you're ready to write the full-blown article. I heard novelist John Grisham say that the outlines for his books are highly detailed. Once he actually starts writing, however, his job is easy because he has a wonderful guide the whole time.

Visualize yourself as a published author—Imagine how the phrase "a published author" will look on your resume. By visualizing the rewards of writing and getting your article published, you can break out of the chains that hold you back and get started on an article that you can finish today.

Clear your workspace—Get rid of everything except what's needed to write your article. People often have trouble writing because their desk or workspace is a mess and not conducive to creativity. Recognize that during the time you're preparing an article you need to tune out distractions. Working on a clear surface is an effective way to do this.

Write for a few minutes—And see what happens. Forget all the excuses. Set an alarm for five minutes, sit down, and start writing. Often you'll find that you don't want to stop after a few minutes. Getting started is the key obstacle to writing productively. If you can master this "few-minute technique," you'll develop a habit that will blast the term "writer's block" out of your vocabulary. This technique is so effective that even if you can't complete the article at the initial sitting, you'll finish faster and more easily than you would have otherwise.

GETTING PUBLISHED AND CAREER OPPORTUNITIES

The benefits you can derive from getting published depend on how you take advantage of it. I don't count on the chance that my target market actually will see and/or remember my articles when they're first published. It's nice when that happens, but the odds are against it. It's more important to make an attractive, professionally produced reprint that you can use in support of your career marketing efforts. Here are action steps you can take:

- Mail reprints to your clients and associates.
- Give copies to your peers, relatives, and friends.
- Talk to the editor immediately to get ideas for further articles you could write for that publication.
- Mention the article (and publication) in your telephone conversations.

GETTING QUOTED

If writing an article is good for your career advancement, think of the benefit that comes from being quoted as an expert by another writer. To do this, contact writers whom you respect, including journalists, columnists, or freelancers, with comments on their articles.

Even criticism, if constructive, may be the basis of a professional relationship with professional writers covering your field. Once you have their respect, offer to send them material they can use in their columns. If you have something interesting to say, there is no reason why they won't use your name.

My pal Robert Bookman lives in Chevy Chase, Maryland, and frequently reads the *Washington Post* "Style Plus" column. He noticed that one of the staff writers, Don Oldenburg, wrote on topics that were particularly intriguing. My friend began a professional, if aggressive, letter-writing campaign to influence Oldenburg to write about Bookman's team productivity programs. Read Bookman's correspondence (Figure 17-3, Three Letters Toward Getting Featured) to learn how to use this tactic with success.

FIGURE 17-3, THREE LETTERS TOWARD GETTING FEATURED

Mr. Don Oldenburg
Style Plus
WASHINGTON POST
1150 15th Street
Washington, D.C. 20071

May 27

Dear Don:

As I mentioned to you over the phone today, I believe my work in the area of teamwork and productivity will be of interest to your readers. I have conducted team productivity programs for some of this city's largest organizations (e.g., American Security Bank, Mitre, Wang Laboratories, U.S. Navy), and have found that the reasons work teams are productive or unproductive do not always show up on organizational charts or yearly reports.

Productivity often depends on people's ability to be able to withstand the hurts that go into mature conflict resolution. I have had the chief executive officer of a major D.C. corporation explain to me that he was reorganizing the corporation simply because he was afraid ("didn't think it was appropriate") to confront a senior vice president. This C.E.O. was not only wasting time with unnecessary reorganizations, but was also creating corporate norms that would hinder team productivity. Healthy corporate norms (cooperation, trust, loyalty, participation) support people's ability to appropriately deal with the strains inherent in all cooperative efforts.

Over the past six years I have accumulated both useful information and amusing anecdotes on how productive teams operate. I think your readers can both benefit from and enjoy what I have learned. I hope to meet with you to further explore the possibility of having Style Plus do a story on my work. Perhaps you would like to hear one of my talks. In two weeks I will be giving a presentation entitled Teamwork: What Those Beer Commercials Don't Tell You! before the American Society of Personnel Administrators.

Could we possibly get together on June 7, or June 8?

Unless I hear from you earlier, I will give you a call on June 4.

Sincerely,

Robert Bookman

Robert Bookman

FIGURE 17-3, THREE LETTERS TOWARD GETTING FEATURED

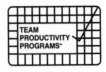

Mr. Don Oldenburg
Style Plus
WASHINGTON POST
1150 15th Street
Washington, D.C. 20071

June 4

Dear Don:

After we spoke today, I started to think about the appeal an article on Team Productivity in STYLE PLUS would have for the general public. Naturally, I think an article on our society's present love affair with the word "team" would have broad appeal.

Our society is mesmerized by this word "team." There's Team Xerox, the NBC News Team, and America's Team—whether it be the Atlanta Braves or Dallas Cowboys. Why is today's vernacular "teeming" with the word team? One major reason is due to the success of Japan's workteam concept. This success is contributing to a shift in the high value we place on rugged individualism to—something else. This something else is often referred to as "teamwork." Yet most Americans (unlike most Japanese) are still uncomfortable with the team concept. Teams, unlike yesterday's officemates, are often short term and require enormous degrees of instant cooperation, trust, loyalty, keeping commitments, acceptance of others, and an "everybody can win attitude." Such qualities usually take quit a bit of time to develop. Yet today's workplace is demanding that we quickly adhere to a new work style.

In essence, I'm suggesting that many people need to be changing their fundamental work style in order to be successful in today's work environment. A problem exists in that many organizations have not informed employees of the new team-oriented work behavior now expected, nor are employees being given the assistance in making those attitudinal and behaviorial changes necessary to conform to such norms. Ten years ago, the norm for getting ahead within most work settings was to "kick a little ass" (as George Bush would say) or to "butter up" the boss. Now the norm is—participate, cooperate, and facilitate the efforts of your fellow teammates. The concept of teamwork sounds easy, but for the majority of Americans, being a member of a team is hard work—damn hard work. The Team Productivity Programs that deliver to major organizations in the D.C. area assist people in obtaining the skills that they need to become successful and well-adjusted team players.

I do hope we can "team up" to do an article. Unless I hear from you earlier, I'll give you a call this coming Tuesday, June 8.

Sincerely,

Robert Bookman

Robert Bookman

FIGURE 17-3, THREE LETTERS TOWARD GETTING FEATURED

Mr. Don Oldenburg
Style Plus
WASHINGTON POST
1150 15th Street
Washington, D.C. 20071

June 20

Dear Don:

The instrument that I gave you indicates that your behavioral characteristics fall into the category of "Persuader." On page seventeen there's a short description of the "Persuader Pattern." A more complete description of this pattern is contained in the enclosed booklet titled: Library of Classical Patterns. Pages one through fourteen of the booklet are merely filler, so I suggest you start reading from page fifteen. Please let me know if you have any questions regarding this material or the instrument.

Don, you said there was good possibility of having your readers be able to get in touch with me by making my telephone number available in the article. My other suggestion was using a photo. You thought that a plain photo of me really wouldn't add to the story, but possibly an "action shot" makes sense. With this possibility in mind, I had several action shots taken last week at a team productivity session I was leading of civilians working with the U.S. Navy. Now, I'm not suggesting you use ALL the photos (!), but perhaps . . .

I think the article on my team productivity work can make an important impact on your readers. It can help them be more productive and less stressful on their job, it can help their organization be more profitable, and it can give employees and employers an understanding of what work styles are most appropriate for success. As you know, a most effective way to get folks to read such an important article is to have a photograph that catches the eye. Don, the instrument you took also categorizes me within the "Persuader Pattern," so how am I doing?

With or without a telephone number here, and a quack quack there, here a photo there a photo everywhere a . . . I wish to thank you for taking the time to consider my initial telephone call, and subsequently write an article on the work that I consider so important.

Looking forward to hearing when the article will appear.

All the best,

Robert Bookman

Robert Bookman

In a matter of weeks a major article appeared in the *Washington Post* featuring Bookman's team productivity program. However, the story doesn't end there. A few weeks after the article appeared, my friend suggested that I contact Don Oldenburg to do a story on me concerning the value of promoting yourself to get ahead in your career. Robert was nice enough to write Don Oldenburg to let him know that I would be making contact. I called Don Oldenburg, followed up with a package of career marketing materials, and followed that up with another call.

Several months went by before he interviewed me. And several more weeks went by before the article was published. Soon enough, however, there it was, splashed across the Style Plus section of the *Washington Post*—an article entitled "Putting Your Best Self Forward," which reflected my 90-minute interview.

Even better, Oldenburg was a member of the *Washington Post* Syndicated Writer's Group, and the article appeared in *hundreds* of other papers across the country. Since the article prominently mentioned my first book, sales picked up nationally and, within its first year, the book was in its third printing.

Is my experience unique? Does it take any special gift to attract this kind of professional recognition and exposure? Not at all. With a little creative thinking and diligent effort, you can achieve the same sort of results for your own career marketing efforts.

BE YOUR OWN PRESS AGENT

What you do is news; perhaps not front page
headline news, but news worthy of mention.
—Jeff Davidson

EVERY MORNING OR EVENING, the local paper features brief news items about professionals in your community. These are often found on the business or financial pages, under town news, or elsewhere in sections such as "People to Watch" or "Names in the News." In Chapter 14, I suggested listing a year in advance all that you hoped to accomplish. You can prepare each item that makes your internal achievements list as a press or news release.

Consider the likely events that will occur in the coming year. You'll probably attend a conference or two. You may have an article published, give a speech, travel abroad, or win an award. You'll be celebrating some type of anniversary, and you'll probably get a raise or promotion. Your local media may consider some or all of these events to be newsworthy.

It's time to become your own press agent and generate significant, positive exposure in the media. Strategic career marketers aiming for the top quickly realize that developing good relations in today's media-driven society isn't optional. Begin collecting the names and addresses of editors and reporters, both locally and nationally, who cover your industry. Add them to your contact management software.

Several directories in Appendix C list the names and addresses of newspapers, magazines, journals, and other periodicals. I maintain several media lists, such as a list of local reporters and publications to whom I send a press release approximately every three to six months. I have another list of editors of national publications in my industry. These include publications such as *Presentations*, *Professional Speaker*, *Sharing Ideas*, *The Executive Speaker*, and *Vital Speeches of the Day*. I also maintain a list of newsletter editors, book reviewers, and fellow authors. Nearly everyone on my list could potentially publish my press releases and articles or mention me in some way.

The local newspaper isn't the only game in town. Your own organization's in-house magazine or newsletter, neighborhood and shopper's guides, church and synagogue bulletins, and local townhouse or condominium newsletters, as well as other publications, are all likely to accept your news releases. Also, online forums are appropriate here. If you have news that fits the format of information services on the Web, go ahead and send your release—but by mail. For some reason, P.R. in the form of e-mail has little impact unless a publisher (online or traditional) invites it.

In many ways, the readership of these alternative or smaller publications can be of greater importance to you, depending on who reads them.

News Releases

Figure 18-1 presents a few of the topics that are suitable for news releases. Start a clipping file of news releases submitted by others that catch your eye and you'll be able to greatly expand to this topic list.

FIGURE 18-1, SUITABLE TOPICS FOR NEWS RELEASES

Your Professional Activities

- Speaking engagements
- Reprint of speeches
- Travel abroad
- Interesting backgrounds, hobbies
- Noteworthy accomplishments
- Appearance on radio or television
- Civic activities
- Elections, appointments
- Courses completed, certificates, degrees
- Seminars attended
- Publications, books, articles
- Mention in trade, professional journals
- Awards, citations, honors

Your Services

- New projects
- Studies completed
- Office expansion, renovation, relocation
- New service introduction
- New uses for existing products

- Lower cost due to more efficient operation
- Unusual service offerings
- Bids or awards
- New contracts

Your Firm

- Affiliation
- Accomplishments
- Anniversaries of firm, principals, or long-term employees
- Association memberships
- New building or radical office change
- Banquets or awards dinners
- Employee training programs
- Projected plans
- Joint programs—government, industry
- website launch, or new website feature

Research

- Survey results
- New discoveries
- Trends, projections, forecasts

SUBMIT AND RETREAT

Once you've made contact with the editors of the various print and online media you have selected, send your news releases on a regular basis, perhaps quarterly. *Never* call the editor, seek a publication date, or ask for clippings. This is the quickest way to guarantee that your news releases will be filed in the trash. Editors are busy people, too, and can't field calls about news or press releases. In the long run, your chances are much better if you simply write a good release and keep quiet. Here are more suggestions on increasing your chances of getting published:

- Lead with who, what, when, where, why, and how.
- Use your full name and title the first time you mention yourself in the release.
- Use a straightforward, easy style with sentences of average length. (I recommend no more than twenty-three words per sentence.)
- Print the news release on clean 8" x 11" paper, placing your phone number in the upper left- or right-hand corner and instructions as to when to use the release in the opposite corner, for instance, "For immediate use" or " For use the week of September 3."
- If the release is more than one page (one page is best), put the word *more* on the bottom of the first page.
- Send a picture, if available.
- Send to the particular department editor if it involves a special interest.

Be accurate. If you aren't, it might be your last chance. The editors to whom you send your release will decide on using your story based on any local angle, general interest, the publication's policy, and timing.

Figures 18-2 and 18-3 contain two releases that were picked up by area press. The first press release was picked up by the *Chapel Hill News,* my current hometown newspaper.

I submitted the second to twelve publications, and three of them carried my story. Remember to scan the papers carefully or you might miss the publication of your own release. Alternatively, use a clipping service such as Luce, Bacon's, or Burrelle's to help gather your published releases.

FIGURE 18-2, PRESS RELEASE IN HOMETOWN NEWSPAPER

Jeff Davidson, CMC ▪ 2417 Honeysuckle Road ▪ Chapell Hill, NC 27514 ▪ (919)932-1996

For Immediate Release

For More Information
Contact: Jeff Davidson
919-932-1996

LOCAL CONSULTANT HAS FIRST BOOK PUBLISHED

Jeff Davidson, a certified management consultant from Falls Church, has co-authored a book which is being shipped this week to major book stores nationwide. The book is entitled *Marketing Your Consulting and Professional Services* and is published by John Wiley & Sons, 605 Third Avenue, New York, NY 10158.

Davidson is a frequent speaker at conventions and seminars offering a wide range of presentations on the management and marketing of professional service firms. As a Certified Management Consultant, a designation awarded by the Institute of Management Consultants, he has obtained the industry's highest accreditation.

He has also authored numerous articles appearing in periodicals and journals, such as *Private Practice, Case and Comment, Real Estate Today, Legal Economics, Dental Management, ABA Banking Journal, Business and Society Review, Professional Insurance Agent, National Public Accountant, Georgetown Law Weekly, Personnel Journal*, and many others.

Davidson has a degree in marketing and an MBA, and is a designated Connecticut State Scholar. He is listed in *Who's Who in Finance and Industry* and *Outstanding Young Men of America*. Previously he was named *the* Washington, D.C., "Small Business Media Advocate of the Year," and an American Institute of Management "Executive of Distinction."

###

FIGURE 18-3, AUTHOR TO VISIT CHINA

Jeff Davidson, CMC ▪ 2417 Honeysuckle Road ▪ Chapell Hill, NC 27514 ▪ (919)932-1996

For Immediate Release

For More Information
Contact: Jeff Davidson
919-932-1996

AUTHOR TO VISIT CHINA

Jeff Davidson, a professional speaker and author from Chapel Hill, North Carolina, will be visiting China this spring to examine problems of entrepreneurship in a state-controlled society. Jeff is author of the book, *Marketing for the Home-Based Business*, Adams Media Inc., Holbrook, MA, publisher, and all told, his books have now sold more than 650,000 copies.

Jeff is a frequent speaker at conventions and seminars, offering a wide range of presentations on *Breathing Space: Living & Working at a Comfortable Pace in a Sped-up Society*. A CMC (Certified Management Consultant awarded by the Institute of Management Consultants), he has obtained his industry's highest accreditation.

Later this year, Jeff will be addressing America Online, IBM, Association Executives of North Carolina, Washington Hospice Center, Professional Secretaries International, American Consulting Foresters, and other groups.

Jeff is one of the nation's most prolific business authors. He has had several thousand articles published in periodicals and journals such as *Sales and Marketing Executive, Personal Selling Power Public Management, Leaders, Association Management, At Your Best, Estate Today, ABA Banking Journal, Business and Society Review, National Public Accountant*, and many others.

###

PHOTO-OPS

I go to a photographer about once every two years and get eight or ten different shots taken. I continually use different pictures on book jackets, magazine articles, and in press releases as part of my strategy to gain exposure and recognition. When you hire a photographer to take your picture, you have several options. One is the head and shoulder shot, which you'll be able to use for virtually all of the promotional vehicles we've discussed. However, you may also want action photos. An action photo might include you in front of a seminar group, receiving an award, or conferring with a colleague. Sometimes action photos can be staged in the photographer's studio. Often they have to be taken on the spot.

Another type of photo is the candid shot, in which you're seated at your desk or in some other environment that gives the reader a sense of your surroundings. Some photographers are equipped to create this type of environment within the studio. Obviously, it's best to check in advance.

KEEP THINGS IN PERSPECTIVE

Only a small percentage of the news releases you submit will be published. Still, the number of free column inches that even one release generates, versus paying for an ad, is quite a coup.

What does getting mentioned in the newspaper do for you? All other things being equal, of any two lawyers, two doctors, or two executives, the one who gets mentioned in the newspaper has the career/professional edge.

There are many ways to leverage your published releases so that they work for you again and again. Similar to when I get an article published, I don't count on anyone in particular seeing my news release when it first appears. If those I'm seeking to influence do see it, I consider that a bonus. Once the release is published, I carefully clip it and make an attractive reprint on good bond paper.

I have now produced a document that I can add to my continuing portfolio of career marketing materials, which includes, by this time, a list of speaker's topics, a published article, and perhaps another person's article in which I'm mentioned. All of these types of materials, plus a bio, fact sheets, photos, and other supporting background information make up the components of what is called a press kit, or for speakers, a presentation kit.

You don't need a big budget to produce a simple, personal, and effective press kit. In fact, if you follow the suggestions in this book, you'll essentially be developing a press kit as you proceed. As you'll see in Chapter 21 (on getting on radio and TV), these materials come in handy in influencing program hosts to invite you as a guest on their shows.

GENERATING PERSONAL PUBLICITY VIA THE WEB

You can use the World Wide Web to effectively market yourself. If you have a website, examine it from the standpoint of how it serves site visitors, as opposed to it making you feel good about yourself and your site. In a nutshell, ensure that your website delivers information that visitors will regard as valuable.

To use your site as a promotional vehicle, you'll employ many of the same types of career marketing techniques that you'd use apart from the Web. Hence, when you write an article, compose a brochure, or prepare a speaker's flyer, mention your website prominently. If you give a speech or an interview, make sure your listeners have ample time to write down your Web address and reason to visit.

Regardless of whether you have a website, you can always drop in on various newsgroups, chat groups, and listservers. Then you can post messages that discreetly allude to something you'd like to make known. You can also contact editors, publishers, and producers to query them regarding your article, announcement, or news item. In each case you would proceed with the professional demeanor and purpose that you'd employ off line.

More Publicity Strategies

If you're willing to spend some money, you might wish to have a logo and personalized stationery developed. This depends on your overall career goals, the type of organization in which you're presently employed, and your personal finances. Designing an original, personalized logo can cost a minimum of $300, not including press and printing fees.

What is a logo? A logo is a pictorial representation of the image you want to create. It can be a picture or design with stylized letters. It needs to be uplifting and present you in a unified way. We have all lived with logos all our lives. The Texaco Star, the Windows 98 "button," the distinctive Coca-Cola script, and even the envelopes we get from the IRS are familiar examples of logos.

SURVEY YOUR GROUP

Strategies in becoming your own press agent include conducting surveys of interest to professionals in your industry. This doesn't have to be complicated. For example, I spoke to the National Capital Speakers Association on the topic of using articles to market your speaking capabilities. The night I was speaking, fifty members and guests attended. As part of my presentation, I invited the group to share with me how I could generate article material in minutes, right before them.

I asked the group how many of them wanted to get published. Fifty hands went up. Then I asked how many had ever been published, and approximately thirty-eight hands went up. How many had used the article to market their speaking capabilities? Twenty-nine hands went up. How many were still using the article as a marketing tool? Fourteen hands went up, and so on. In other words, in speaking to a group of Washington, D.C., area speakers, I was then able to produce a survey-type article entitled "Using Articles to Market Your Speaking Capabilities," which cited actual statistics based on a captive audience survey.

Similarly, I surveyed the area's management consultants. Such surveys are of great interest to the press. You can submit them as articles *or* as news releases. If you submit them as news releases, the first sentence might read, "Author and professional speaker Jeff Davidson recently surveyed fifty local management consultants on how they use articles to market their practice . . ."

TAKE IT IN STRIDE

Sure, all of the above takes work. However, you can handle it all without disrupting your full-time job responsibilities. Figure 18-4 depicts a hypothetical week in the life of a career marketer.

The immense impact and importance of the media today is often misunderstood. One Sunday edition of The *New York Times* bombards us with more information than an average person of a century ago was exposed to in his or her entire lifetime. Today there are more than 12,000 publications listed in *Bacon's Magazine Directory,* and other similar directories covering every possible interest group. Some 99 percent of American households have one or more television sets, and radio has a good deal of impact also. There are ten times as many radio stations today as when television was first developed.

Although you may have not considered it before, taking the time now to plan your media strategy and establishing good relationships with the media will prove invaluable in your future career marketing efforts.

Always be truthful and maintain integrity when dealing with the media. The relationship and reputation you maintain with these keepers of public opinion will grow in importance as your career star continues to rise.

FIGURE 18-3, A STRATEGIC CAREER MARKETER'S CALENDAR NOTES

	SUNDAY	MONDAY	TUESDAY	WEDNESDAY	THURSDAY	FRIDAY	SATURDAY
AM	Read and clip newspaper articles and items of interest.		Discuss project plans with boss.		Listen to motivational cassette during commute.		
LUNCH		Meet with peers for lunch.		Meet with higher-up for lunch.		Review job & career marketing tasks for next week.	
PM	Note: Once a month update internal achievements list, volunteer for a community project, send action letters.						
EVENING	Talk to key individuals and meet with a mentor or career coach.	Scan professional journals. Add to clip file. Call colleagues network.	Speak to a local group or work on an article. Attend seminar.	Stay late at work to help a colleague.		Stop off at company watering hole.	

CERTIFICATION AND YOUR CAREER

Try not to become a man of success but rather try to become a man of value.

—Albert Einstein

IN CONTEMPORARY SOCIETY, we look to certification and licensing as a way of judging the credentials and experience of a professional. It lets us know that the professionals we hire have passed certain examinations or qualifications set by their industry. Institutionalized license procedures such as "M.D." tell us that the person has completed the training necessary to meet standards set by law. Dentists have D.D.S. after their names, indicating successful completion of training and an examination. A Certified Public Accountant (C.P.A.) signifies a certification of quality in the profession of accounting.

"In our observations as futurists," say Roger Herman and Joyce Gioia, strategic business futurists specializing in workforce and workplace trends, "we've seen the rising importance of certifications. Becoming legitimately certified in a particular field or specialty is a smart way to validate your credentials and to differentiate yourself from competitors."

You may be interested in getting certified in your field. What are the career advancement benefits, however, of being certified? What kinds of professions provide certification? Are there any directories that can be used to identify associations and societies that offer certification programs in your field?

WHAT DOES CERTIFICATION MEAN?

Certification is frequently confused with accreditation and/or licensing.

Accreditation applies to programs rather than individuals, generally those of a school, college, institute, or university. It's granted by an association to organizations that meet standards determined through initial and periodic evaluations.

Licensing applies to individuals and is granted by a political body to people who meet predetermined qualifications. It's required by law before certain professionals, such as doctors and dentists, can practice those occupations.

Certification also applies to individuals. It's voluntarily granted by an association to people who meet predetermined qualifications.

INVESTIGATE BEFORE ALL ELSE

Herman and Gioia, who are based in Greensboro, North Carolina, and on the Web at http://www.herman.net, suggest that you investigate certification programs carefully before accepting the value of the certification itself. "Evaluate whether the certification process is rigorous enough to be valid. Inquire about the requirements for re-certification to validate continuing expertise."

"Anyone can declare himself a certifying body and attract people hungry for recognition. Be careful. In our field of management consulting, for example, there are many profit-making organizations offering to certify consultants for a price. Only the

Institute of Management Consultants is a legitimate professional organization offering the Certified Management Consultant (CMC) designation," say Herman and Gioia, both of whom are CMCs.

More than 300 associations and societies have professional certification programs in place. In no particular order, here is a sampling of certification programs:

FIGURE 19-1, AN ARRAY OF CERTIFICATIONS

Certificate for Welding Inspectors
Certificate in Data Processing
Certification and Qualification of Quality Control Inspectors
Certification for Occupational Therapy Assistants
Certified Association Executive
Certified Commercial Investment Member
Certified Life Underwriter
Certified Hospitality Housekeeping Executive
Certified Human Resource Executive
Certified Business Communicator
Certified Catering Executives
Certified Corporate Travel Executive
Certified Exposition Manager
Certified Engineering Operations Executive
Certified Speech Pathologist
Certified Telecommunications Consultant
Certified Hospitality Supervisor
Certified Hotel Sales Executive
Certified Incentive Travel Executive

Certified Meeting Professional
Council of Peers Award of Excellence
Certified Tour Professional
Certified Trade Show Marketer
Certified Electronics Technician
Certified Financial Planner
Certified Laboratory Assistant
Certified Purchasing Manager
Certified Room Division Executive
Certified Special Events Professional
Certified Travel Counselor
Certified Military Club Manager
Certified Professional Social Worker
Certified Safety Professional
Certified Speaking Professional
Certified Food and Beverage Executives
Certified Hotel Administrator
Certified Professional Secretary
Certified Meeting Professional
Certified Management Consultant
Certified Public Accountant
Certified Massage Therapist
Certified Shorthand Reporter

To find who offers the certification in your field, call the most prominent association serving your profession or industry, and simply ask. If you don't know the most prominent association, check Appendix A: Professional Trade Associations on page 216 of this book. Two directories list thousands of professional, trade, and technical associations and societies that offer certification programs. You can find them in the reference section of your local library:

- *Gale's Directory of Associations*
- *National Trade and Professional Associations*

Locate the group in your field and request detailed information about any certification programs available.

NOT FOR THE MEEK

In most industries, the certification process involves taking an examination, signing a written code of ethics, and describing your complete professional experience. Many industries also recertify members periodically as a way of helping them keep pace with new developments in their fields.

The certification process is necessarily rigorous. Many professionals complain about certification procedures as "jumping through too many hoops," but they know the process of applying and earning acceptance is essential for a truly professional designation. After all, if it were easy to become certified, the certification would be worth little to its recipients and their clients.

Herman and Gioia predict that certifications will become so narrow "that the experienced generalist dedicated to gaining validation of credentials may accumulate a rather long list of initials to add to business cards." As an example, they cite certification offered by George Mason University and a sponsoring organization called the Connected International Meeting Professionals Association.

When I heard of this designation, the Certified Internet Meeting Professional, I thought, "Gee, nearly anyone could qualify." However, applicants have to be certified previously by a recognized professional organization in the field, earning designations already widely accepted, such as CCM, CICM, CMP, CMM, CAE, or CEM.

A CERTIFICATION JOURNEY

When I began management consulting fresh out of the University of Connecticut's MBA program, I had no idea that I would soon start working toward career certification. After a year, however, things I'd been hearing led me to write to the Institute for Management Consultants to inquire about their Certified Management Consultant (CMC) designation.

When I realized how rigorous the process was, I was motivated to work that much harder for certification. The requirements then included five years of experience as a management consultant and at least one as a project manager. The applicant had to submit five client mini-cases, including a description of a client engagement in complete detail, three client references, and three associate references. In addition, there was an interview by a panel of three CMCs, an application fee, an initiation fee, and annual dues.

I learned that one-third of the Certified Management Consultants came from large national consulting firms (like McKinsey & Company and Lawrence Leiter and Associates). Another third came from major management advisory services, such as Price Waterhouse; and KPMG, Peat, and Marwick. Few, such as myself, were from smaller firms. Nevertheless, as soon as I had the required years of experience, I applied.

It took me nine months to complete the process and be granted certification. At the tender age of 31, I was accepted. I knew I had earned my CMC designation, but I also knew that it was up to me to reap the greatest possible benefits from it (see Figure 19-1).

FIGURE 19-2, PROFESSIONAL CERTIFICATION

Like accountants and architects, management consultants have a professional organization—the Institute of Management Consultants—that certifies individuals who voluntarily submit to its accreditation process and meet strict membership requirements.

To be a Certified Management Consultant, or CMC, a consultant must have a proven track record of superior client service and must demonstrate a high level of professional competence before a qualifying panel of his peers.

Ethically, a CMC pledges to place client interests first; to maintain objectivity and independence of position at all times; to safeguard client information; and to accept only those assignments that will result in real benefit to the client.

Institute certification is a valuable aid to management in the quest for competent consulting. It's the mark of a professional.

 INSTITUTE OF MANAGEMENT CONSULTANTS
521 5th Avenue 35th Fl
New York, NY 10175-3598
212-697-8262

PERKS OF CERTIFICATION

Certification programs offer benefits for the individuals receiving certification, as well as for the associations that bestow them. For individuals, here are some of the primary benefits:

Distinction—When you can use a designated certification label with your name, people inside and outside your organization or profession recognize that you have a certain degree of expertise in your field. Although they may not know anything about the certification requirements or the certifying association, they almost automatically determine that you're a serious, noteworthy professional.

Recognition on the job—It's often difficult to get the attention of top management for the work you do. Certification provides a chance for junior-level professionals to get noticed.

Access to colleagues—Certification provides you with scheduled occasions to become involved with the certifying association—attend conferences, speak at meetings, or simply have a common ground for discussions with others who are also certified. Often, this generates a professional network of colleagues who will be some of your best contacts for advice, information, and especially active support if you are job shopping.

Certification programs also prove beneficial to employers. The president of one management consulting firm only looks at resumes of people who have a CMC. "It's a quick way for me to know immediately who is worth talking to," he says.

Information exchange—Involvement with other certified professionals allows you to keep up with the latest developments in your field and establish channels for an interchange of information that crosses organizational boundaries. This has important implications for career development, as you become more aware of the various options for employment for individuals in your profession.

Staying sharp—Because you are exposed to top professionals in your field, you're encouraged to keep your knowledge and abilities current. You may do this by attending seminars and conferences offered through the certifying associations or by reading the newsletters, magazines, and other publications the association may distribute.

Reassess your career—The process of applying for certification can be a valuable self-assessment and development tool as you prepare for the certifying examination and/or review your achievements in writing for the application. Many certifications require periodic updating, which allows you continued opportunities for reassessing your professional strengths and weaknesses.

Leadership position—Not everyone in your field will be certified. Your certification places you in a natural leadership position in your profession, giving you valuable visibility among those in your own field, as well as outside it.

MAKE IT WORK FOR YOU

All these benefits, of course, are only as valuable as you make them. You have to *use* your certification. Add your designation to your stationery and business cards. Ensure that it's included when anything is written about you. Volunteer to serve on committees and speak at the meetings of your certifying association. Submit written items to their publications. Take a leadership role in organizing and conducting any local meetings of professionals in your field. Get involved and stay involved to make your certification work for you in major ways.

As a professional, you have every right and many reasons to seek certification.

THE EFFECT OF VIDEO PRESENTATIONS ON YOUR FUTURE

You grow up the day you have your first real laugh—at yourself.

—Edith Barrymore

WHETHER ON A VIDEO RESUME, a real-video broadcast on your website, a half-hour interview on a local cable television program, a taped presentation on company benefits to new employees, or a three-minute spot on *Good Morning America,* chances are good that video skills will come in handy in your career marketing.

My first introduction to video came years ago when I took a community college course. At six-foot-three and 184 pounds, I'd always feared that on video I'd come across long and lanky. To my great surprise, I was actually satisfied with how I appeared, and this certainly served as a confidence booster.

Later, after I began speaking professionally, I videotaped presentations as marketing tools. I procured other speaking engagements by letting meeting planners view previous presentations. The tape was also valuable for self-assessment purposes. Seeing yourself on videotape is seeing yourself in a brand-new way. Sure, you own a camcorder, but have you actually used it to enhance your career?

You Can Sparkle on Screen

The *Harvard Business Review* long ago predicted that media presentation skills would be required of most managers and executives. Bert Decker, founder and president of Decker Communications in San Francisco, notes that video training has many applications, but is most valuable in giving personal feedback to help individual performance. Professionals in all fields can benefit from polished video skills.

Such skills may already be widely used within your organization, through teleconferencing, online training, videotaped product demonstrations, public information programs, and other creative applications. As we see greater use of television, video, and real-video to communicate in all businesses, the need for these skills will intensify.

If well-prepared, you can accept this new situation with confidence and be able to deliver a powerful, "larger-than-life" presentation. However, expert Maggie Bedrosian says that without the necessary training and experience on video, most speakers surrender the challenge to "the other person."

Suppose that your industry calls for proposals to present information on a massive international teleconference. You realize that you could reach 30,000 people worldwide who are interested in your specialty or field of expertise. Are you ready to volunteer?

What if you have a new product line to introduce to your sales team across the country and around the world, or an orientation program to conduct monthly at scattered sites? In these instances, you want to ensure that everyone receives the same complete, accurate information. You can also prepare intensively for one high-impact program which can be used repeatedly. Video lets you guarantee the uniformity of your presentations.

Companies can afford to use their most productive and dynamic presenters. Whether a session is conducted in Hackensack, New Jersey, or Budapest, Hungary, all participants receive the same basic information. Are you involved in producing custom-tailored presentations for your organization?

Alternatively, a video resume or online video feature functions as a powerful preliminary screening before possible meetings. Could you convince an unseen potential employer/client of your skills via these communication vehicles?

PREPPING FOR THE CAMERA

The audience responds to your message at many levels, so getting ready for the camera is important. Obviously, the audience can hear you speak, but more importantly, they can see you.

"Our impact on our audience is conveyed not only in our choice of words," according to Bert Decker, "but in how we say them." When properly controlled, the body is an amazing tool for communications. The art of mime is a strong example.

Perhaps the best way to evaluate overall physical communication is one "piece" at a time, beginning with the head. These tips will also be helpful for television appearances.

Face up to your face—Your most important "televehicle" is your face. Don't worry about being overly expressive, or that your nose, teeth, and eyes are off center. Except for Mel Gibson and Denzel Washington, there are almost no symmetrical faces in the world. Picture Katharine Hepburn, Albert Einstein, Tom Hanks, Lee Iacocca, Ronald Reagan—expressive faces, not symmetrical faces.

You may want to accept makeup if it's offered before facing the camera. Fran Campbell, a specialist in this area, reports that both men and women can reap these benefits from TV makeup:

- Because the lights and camera tend to flatten your features, makeup enhances your natural features.
- Makeup helps you look healthy, vital, and alert, which encourages viewers to be more attentive.
- A light dusting of translucent powder reduces the glare and sweat caused by studio lights. This replaces that nervous-sweaty look with one of relaxed assurance.

If makeup isn't offered, do it yourself. Women may use their regular makeup, but apply it a bit more heavily. You don't need the drama of stage makeup—just a hint beyond everyday use. Both men and women may want to carry baby powder or another translucent powder and a large brush for applying it. If you're under the lights for a long period, check your "shine" level on each break. You can freely apply many layers of translucent powder before it shows.

Your attire—Let your clothes underline your message, not argue with it; let what you choose to wear reinforce what you choose to say. People react to what you wear and how you wear it as well as to your words. Whether this is an artificial or hypocritical standard isn't the issue. People respond to what they see and judge accordingly. Appropriate clothes on video are those that support, or at least don't distract from, your message. Because of the way the camera functions, author Maggie Bedrosian advises that it's best to *avoid*:

- Stark white, red, or black in large quantity, as these colors bloom, bleed, or wash out on camera.
- Large, bold, high contrast designs or prints, as they scream for attention, upstaging you and your ideas.

- Large metallic decorations or jewelry, as they reflect lights or create distracting noises.
- Narrow, repeating stripes, such as herringbone, as they wave and weave on camera.

However, it is good to *choose*:

- Subdued or neutral colors appropriate to your style and skin tone.
- A comfortable fit sitting or standing.
- Fuller skirts for women for ease of walking and attractive drape when sitting.
- Simple, clean necklines that don't interfere with microphone placement.

Glasses—It's better, if possible, not to wear glasses on camera. You may, however, wish (or need) to wear them for two reasons. First, you may need them to see the host or to read. Second, people may be accustomed to seeing you in glasses, and they may not recognize you without them. If you do need glasses, wear those with nonglare rims. Ask the video technician if he/she has a nonglare spray. The director might ask you to tilt the glasses down a fraction to reduce the glare. This may feel clumsy to you, but it's less distracting than glare.

Making contact—Bedrosian offers these few guidelines for eye contact with the camera:

1. The camera can be an eavesdropper. Usually you'll be looking at the reporter, the other panelists, or the questioner while the camera eavesdrops. You don't need to look into the camera, and, in fact, it's better if you don't. You're supposed to "ignore" the camera in such a situation. If an interview lasts more than five minutes, you may find yourself talking to your partner—who turns away for a word with the stage manager or to take a sip

of water. If this happens, keep natural eye contact with the reporter, who isn't even there! Your real audience is the unseen viewer, not the people in the studio. Keep your poise for that real audience.

2. The camera can be a listener. Use direct eye contact with the camera only when you're talking directly to the audience. You can blink, but return to the camera—the "eyes" of your audience. This can be difficult because it's contrary to normal speaking patterns. In our society, the listener generally maintains eye contact while the speaker may look away, look down, or even close his or her eyes in thought. In direct eye contact for video, those natural motions are distracting, so address the camera with your eyes.

3. The camera can be "one of the gang." Sometimes the camera is located in the studio audience or in the group of people you're addressing. In that case, you maintain eye contact with the camera as if it were another audience member. Don't focus exclusively on it; make brief contact as you would with any audience member.

Gestures—Studios sometimes tell guests to "sit on their hands." This overstates the point that television is an intimate medium. The camera picks up slight nuances of expression and gesture, both of which convey powerful impact. Your TV appearance is not theater, so no need for sweeping motions, pounding fists, and other dramatic gestures, which can interfere with your message.

Use natural gestures. Imagine a barrier six inches below your shoulders and keep your hands below that level unless you have a particularly strong reason for being dramatic. Reassure yourself that this small-scale and intimate quality of video makes it a potent medium for people of spirit and conviction who might never otherwise address large audiences.

Handling an Interview

The video or television opportunity with the greatest potential for marketing oneself is the interview show. You could appear on or host a local cable program or be a guest on a broadcast talk show. Your segment may run from three minutes to an hour, but the main guidelines, according to Bedrosian, remain the same:

- Present yourself as clearly and cleanly as possible.
- Don't go on to "sell" your specific product or service.
- Drawing from a keen sense of humor or a unique talent will further color your personality and bring life to an otherwise ordinary interview.

STAY COOL

How you look on camera is not entirely up to you. Lighting, camera angles, the setting the director selects—all of these have great impact on how you appear in the final product. Rarely do you have control in these areas. If invited, you want to see yourself on the monitor, request a certain placement of lights, or ask to be filmed in a setting reflecting your work. Ordinarily, however, trust the professionals and don't fret about technical details.

People who are confident in their ability to communicate can do so more easily. This is the overall goal of video training. Tomorrow's executive will have a wealth of video technology at his or her fingertips from video-conferencing, to Internet training, to high definition production to desktop video, to videophones. Your success depends on your preparation today.

APPEARING ON TV AND RADIO

Don't be humble: You're not that great.
— Golda Meir

R
ADIO AND TELEVISION ARE NATURAL MEDIA FOR self-promotion. The people responsible for programming what goes out over the airwaves generally welcome the chance to consider new ideas and information. This is especially true for the talk shows that rely on interviewing people who can provide interesting discussions on timely topics.

Consider the statistics. There are more than 10,000 radio stations; between ten and thirty in most cities in the United States. Each metropolitan area also has about three to five local television stations in addition to the national networks. Not all the programming is entertainment or news; there are more than 45,000 radio, television, and cable talk shows and at least two dozen regular talk shows in any given metropolitan area, not to mention those also available to viewers with cable, Prime Star, or DirecTV connections. These talks shows may be daily or weekly, and their hosts are constantly seeking people who have expertise and/or opinions in a wide variety of areas.

This means that, arithmetically, getting on radio and TV isn't so difficult. It helps to understand the business, however, and carefully plan your approach.

TALK SHOWS

Each year, more than two million guests are scheduled to appear on legitimate programs (not Jerry Springer or Ricki Lake) broadcast throughout the United States and Canada. You don't need to be a celebrity or even known at all—approximately 90 percent of all radio and TV talk show guests are "common" folk, virtually unknown to the listening or viewing audience before they speak.

Although some people take great pains and preparation before appearing on a show and hire agents or publicists, many media consultants agree that, with some information and a little effort, you can do a good job without paying a small fortune for coaching. I recommend that you get a couple of books, tapes, or articles on how to appear on radio or TV and read them before appearing as a guest.

Brian Jud, president of the Book Authority, has several resources on the topic. E-mail: Jud@marketingdirections.com. Also, my own 6-cassette album, *Selling Yourself: Strategies for Successful Self-Promotion,* offers many insights on getting on shows and being a big hit. Visit http://www.BreathingSpace.com for details.

GETTING A FOOT IN THE DOOR

My experience with getting on radio and TV is probably indicative of the way it's happened or can happen for many professionals. My first experience came as a result of teaching an adult education course. A radio station host saw my course in the catalog and called to ask me for an interview. I did the interview, and not a lot happened as a result. I asked for a copy of the tape so I could review it and improve my oral presentation. I found it helpful to be able to hear myself, and I decided on ways to say things differently the next time. Also, hearing the tape gave me new angles on the information I'd presented, and I was able to convert it into a magazine article.

As I wrote more articles and gained more expertise to share with listening audiences, I developed a list of radio talk show hosts whose programs might be appropriate for me. I also developed packages of materials—"mini" press kits—to send to hosts. These indicated my background and the subjects I could address on the air. I got selected for about two shows for every fifteen packages I sent out.

After I had been on six or eight radio talk shows, a program assistant at CBS Television saw one of my articles on career marketing and asked me to be on "CBS Nightwatch with Charlie Rose." I appeared on four separate segments, including one on working with a difficult boss and another on strategies for career marketing. From those appearances, I received invitations to be on more shows and also obtained a videotape of my segments for my own review. When I began writing books, my radio and TV appearances accelerated.

"EXPOSING YOURSELF" PAYS OFF

Getting on radio and television has a way of spiraling—the more exposure you get, the more shows you're asked to be on. Only you can take the first steps of identifying the shows and topics and offering your services.

No matter what field you're in, and whether you work for an organization or are self-employed, you can reap immediate benefits from being on radio and TV. People who know you, through your work or outside your work, will eventually hear or see you, or at the least, they'll learn that you were on a show. This means that they're likely to grant you a greater amount of professional credibility than they did previously, and they're likely to give greater credit to your ideas and opinions. Your exposure and visibility broaden beyond your current position.

You may get some feedback from people who hear you on radio or watch you on TV. When you get good feedback, it helps your self-confidence and reminds you about your strengths. When you get less favorable feedback, you begin to see yourself in the eyes of others and you get an opportunity to work on correcting problems—don't shortchange it.

Always ask for a video or an audio tape following your appearances. Reviewing them will give you a chance at self-correction. Assess your voice. Was it too nasal? Too high-pitched? Did you sound authoritative enough? How about your content? Did you ramble? Were you vague rather than precise? Did you leave out any key points? Did you talk in terms that viewers or listeners could readily understand?

A good host often brings out the best in you. You find yourself saying things in ways you haven't said them before, and this opens up new ideas and insights. When reviewing a tape from a show on which I've appeared, I always gain new ways of looking at my areas of professional interest. Frequently, this leads to new ideas for articles or even books.

THE TOPIC AND THE SHOW

With so many radio and TV talk shows in a given locale, you may find it difficult to determine the ones that would be appropriate for you. Start with the shows you know. Those that you already watch or listen to are likely to be the shows with audiences that might want to hear from you. Next, cancel out the shows that are unlikely—those that may specialize in areas outside your field or those with the wrong format. That still leaves many programs which you may not know about.

Your newspaper program guide is a good place to find out about other potential shows. Your local Chamber of Commerce is likely to have a list of local stations and shows as well. And that list may also include the names of programming contacts you'll need to approach with your ideas for your appearances.

To get into talk shows in a big way, purchase the *Talk Show Selects*, by Mitchell P. Davis. It's one of the most widely used talk show directories available, updated frequently, with department heads and direct contact information.

Broadcast Interview Source
2233 Wisconsin Avenue, N.W. # 301
Washington, DC 20007-4104
1-800-YEARBOOK

Also, the list of radio and television station directories presented below will provide you with the names and addresses of thousands of media leads. However, they can be a tad expensive.

Radio and Television Station Directories

Broadcasting/Cable Casting Yearbook
Broadcasting Publications, Inc.
1735 De Sales Street, NW
Washington, DC 20036
(Every radio, TV, and cable outlet in the United States is listed; this is the bible of the broadcasting industry.)

Working Press of the Nation
National Research Bureau
310 South Michigan Avenue
Chicago, IL 60604
(A five-directory set of newspapers, magazines, TV and radio, feature writers, and internal publications. A good overall media guide.)

Public Relations Plus
P.O. Box 329
Washington Depot, CT 06794
(Offers five directories: *New York Publicity Directory, Metro California Media, TV Publicity Outlets Nationwide, Cable TV Publicity Outlets* and *The Family Page Directory*.)

Radio Programming Profile
BF Communications, Inc.
40 Railroad Avenue
Glen Head, NY 00545
(Three times a year, publishes large-market and small-market volumes of talk show contact information.)

Larimi Radio Contacts
Larimi Communications
Associates
151 East 50th Street
New York, NY 10022
(Provides names and addresses
of 3,000 local, network, and
syndicated radio shows featuring guest interviews. One
thousand and one hundred
pages in the annual edition with
a monthly update.)

Cable Services Report
Local Programming National
Cable Association
1724 Massachusetts Avenue,
NW
Washington, DC 20036
(Provides names and addresses
of more than 800 cable televi-
sion systems throughout the
United States.)

Once you have a decent list, watch and listen to as many shows
as possible. If there's some doubt as to whether a show is appropriate for you, assume it is until you know otherwise. That is,
approach producers or hosts at that show with your ideas and materials, and let them decide.

FIND YOUR TOPIC AND ANGLE

Determining the topics, including the specific angle that you
might want to discuss on a radio or TV show, may seem a bit
difficult at first, but it does get easier as you become more
familiar with what is wanted and with what you have to offer.
Obviously, you need to examine your own areas of experience,
expertise, and special knowledge first. You'll need to think about
an angle—some aspects of your knowledge or expertise that
would make it all the more interesting to a listening or viewing
audience. Below are some ideas:

- New angle—does your expertise lend itself to in-depth discussion of something currently in the news?
- Trend angle—could your expertise enable you to shed light
  on a current trend or identify a new one?

- Local angle—does your expertise put you in the position of being a "local" spokesperson on a topic of national significance?
- Controversy angle—has your expertise led you to opinions that are on one side or the other of a stimulating public debate?

Be creative when you formulate your topics. Develop as many ideas as possible in areas that you can discuss with authority. When you put your mind to it, you'll find you have more to say than you think. For example, maybe you had to research the impact of a new municipal tax on your company. Now you're in a position to discuss its general impact on air. Or, maybe your work in the area of financial management has given you some good ideas for tips on how people can streamline their personal financial management. Offer to share these on radio and TV.

ASSESSING PUBLIC ACCESS TELEVISION

Public television is a good outlet for getting initial exposure, practicing your approach, and testing your ideas. If your community has cable TV, then it has public access channels that create free air time for community groups and citizens.

Cable operators have to provide these and allow groups and individuals to air messages. They allow you to develop your own program, using one or more video cameras at the public access studios. The resources aren't extensive and your production expertise is probably limited, so you'll want to keep anything you produce for public access as simple as possible, even an interview with one other person.

To get on public access television, find the administering body. Often this is the local cable company, or it may be a municipal agency. You'll need to work closely with the administering body to develop your program and schedule your air time. If you find that your ideas for a program fit within their guidelines, your efforts may be well worth it. At the least, you get experience and a good deal of knowledge about production and programming.

REMEMBER YOUR PRESS KIT

Once you've targeted some shows and have developed some likely topics, you'll need to assemble the items we've discussed throughout this book into a press kit to send to the show producers and/or hosts. As previously discussed, this is a package of written material (preferably presented in an attractive folder) that tells media sources what you *have done* and what you *can do* on a show (see Chapter 18).

Items that you can use in your press kit include:

- Biography (a bio or other chronology of your experience as it pertains to what you would present on radio and TV).
- Clips (samples of any pertinent material you've authored).
- Articles that mention you.
- Press releases (news about you).
- Media contact sheet (list of previous media contacts, including print media).
- Position paper (a statement by you that indicates your viewpoints on the topic you would discuss).
- Letters of endorsement.
- Photographs (for television press kits).
- Fact sheets, brochures.

When you send your press kit, include a personalized cover letter for the show host or media outlet. Briefly summarize why you'd make a great talk show guest, what topic you have in mind, and where you can be reached for scheduling.

If you're in a large metropolitan area with many radio and television stations and shows, you may want to consider having your material sent out by a media mailing service. The same is true if you get to the point where you feel you need regional or national coverage. Such services can develop a list for your materials and mail them out for you. Many will also do the duplicating and collating work for your press kit.

If you're sending out your own press kit materials, don't send them to the stations with a "Dear Sirs," or a "To whom it may concern" letter. Call the station and find out exactly who is responsible for making decisions concerning the show you have in mind. It may be the show's host, or it may be the producer or a programming director. Send your kit and address your cover letter directly to that person. Your materials are much more likely to get attention and the recipient is more likely to feel your request merits a response.

Make follow-up phone calls within about three days after your mailing. Be prepared to summarize your ideas in a few words for those who might not have read your press kit. Also, think of any additional information you might add at this point—"plugs" that could make your ideas seem all the more interesting. Sometimes, and you have to "sense" when, it's best to call first to generate interest, then mail, then call again.

Organize a file concerning your mailings—names and addresses of individual recipients, cover letters, and notes about responses. Review this file from time to time and let it be a "tickler" to remind you when you haven't had a response after several weeks.

DO YOUR HOMEWORK

There is a mystique about radio and television that makes many people think it applies only to "performers"—those individuals who have an ability to entertain and interest the audience. Yet, if you start watching and listening to talk shows, you'll realize that most of the people interviewed have no performance background at all. Instead, they've figured out how to package themselves and their messages in an informative way. This is something that, with a little effort and patience you can do, too.

When you're asked to be on television or radio, watch or listen to the particular show as much as possible prior to ground zero to familiarize yourself with the format and the host's personality. This will give you an idea of the types of questions asked and whether you'll be doing a monologue-type discussion or simply giving brief answers.

Develop your own list of likely questions and answers, and rehearse them. Contemplate the key points you want to make. How will you make them if you aren't asked a question about them directly? Try simply inserting into the conversation a statement that begins with, "I am often asked . . ." Then, you can go on to answer your own questions.

Part of your preparation involves thinking about the personality you want to project. Do you want to be viewed as authoritative, forceful, intellectual, humorous, or what? When you see others who come across this way, what do they say and do? It helps to identify radio and television role models whose styles you can emulate and adapt as your own. Also, the tips and suggestions in Chapter 20 on using video are useful in preparation for your radio or TV appearance.

Once you've determined your style and developed a list of questions and answers, rehearse on audiotape, on video, or in front of your mirror. You could be amazed at how much self-correction you might do before you go on the air. The reassurance of knowing you're well rehearsed, however, will help you stay relaxed and self-confident when you appear.

POST-SHOW CONSIDERATION

Ask for a tape after the show. It will help you immensely for future radio and television appearances. If things went well, ask for a letter of thanks. You might feel a little hesitant asking for such a letter, but if you can include a letter or two from an ABC affiliate or perhaps CNN in your press kit, your next talk show visit may follow quickly. Keep in touch with the people at the show where you appeared and send *them* a letter of thanks after your appearance. Later, contact them later with ideas for future appearances.

MAKING THE MOST OF MEDIA APPEARANCES

By now you know how the strategic career marketer leverages exposure for use again and again. Following your media appearance on radio or TV, I recommend duplicating your audio or video tape if you are pleased with it, so that you can then send it to others, thereby increasing your chances of being invited to be a guest elsewhere. Also, as previously mentioned, review the tapes carefully and see if you surprise yourself with any new thoughts, ideas, or angles related to the work that you do or the services you provide.

Have the tape transcribed and then carefully determine if you can fashion an article or two from the transcription. Log in the date, time, and topic of this most recent media appearance on your media contact sheet so that your personal press kit always remains up-to-date. Finally, reflect on your career marketing goals, and how your most recent media appearance can help accelerate those goals.

Professional exposure is your ticket to the rest of the world. Before reading this book, if you hadn't taken step one toward strategically marketing your career, all this may have seemed a bit overwhelming. Once you get started, or if you've already started, you quickly see how small career marketing victories add up and help you to experience an upward spiral that never needs to stop.

Perhaps the best definition of success—certainly career success—that I've encountered is from South Carolina speaker Al Walker, who defines it as "making the most of the best that is within you every day by having a goal, being committed to it, and underscoring it with enthusiasm."

The work that you do, and the services that you provide, can make a difference. Strategic career marketing will help to expose others to the good you're already doing.

PROFESSIONAL TRADE ASSOCIATIONS

COMMUNICATIONS, GRAPHICS, PRINTING

American Association of Advertising
Agencies
Chrysler Building
405 Lexington Avenue
New York, NY 10174-1801
Phone 212-682-2500
Fax 212-953-5665

Direct Marketing Association
1120 Avenue of the Americas
New York, NY 10036-6700
Phone 212-768-7277
Fax 212-302-6714

Graphic Communications
International Union
1900 L Street, 9th Floor, NW
Washington, DC 20036
Phone 202-462-1400
Fax 202-331-9516

International Association of Business
Communicators
1 Hallidie Plaza, #600
San Francisco, CA 94102-2818
Phone 415-433-3400
Fax 415-362-8762

Small Publishers Association of
North America
P.O. Box 1306
425 Cedar Street
Buena Vista, CO 81211-1306
Phone 719-395-4790
Fax 719-395-8374

Printing Industries of America
100 Daingerfield Road
Alexandria, VA 22314
Phone 703-519-8100
Fax 703-548-3227

Public Relations Society of America
33 Irving Place, 3rd Floor
New York, NY 10003-2376
Phone 212-995-2230
Fax 212-995-0757

COMPUTERS, DATA PROCESSING

American Electronics Association
5201 Great American Parkway
Suite 520
Santa Clara, CA 95054
Phone 800-284-4232
Fax 408-970-8565

Information Industry Association
1625 Massachusetts Avenue NW
Suite 700
Washington, DC 20036
Phone 202-968-0280
Fax 202-638-4403

Society for Information Management
401 N Michigan Avenue
Suite 2200
Chicago, IL 60611
Phone 312-644-6610
Fax 312-245-1081

Association of Information Technology
Professionals
505 Busse Highway
Park Ridge, IL 60068
Phone 800-224-9371
Fax 847-825-1693

CONSTRUCTION, CONTRACTING

Associated Builders & Contractors, Inc.
1300 N 17th Street
Roslyn, VA 22209
Phone 703-812-2000
Fax 703-812-8203

Associated General Contractors of
America
1957 E Street, NW
Washington, DC 20006
Phone 202-393-2040
Fax 202-347-4004

National Association of Home Builders
1201 15th Street, NW
Washington, DC 20005
Phone 202-822-0200
Fax 202-822-0559

National Association of the
Remodeling Industry
403 N. Fairfax Drive, Suite 310
Arlington, VA 22203
Phone 703-276-7600
Fax 703-243-3465

American Society of Appraisers
555 Herndon Parkway, Suite 125
Herndon, VA 22070
Phone 703-478-2228
Fax 703-742-8471

American Society of Professional
Estimators
11141 Georgia Avenue, #412
Wheaton, MD 20902
Phone 301-929-8848
Fax 301-929-0231

Building Owners and Managers
Association International
1201 New York Avenue, Suite 300
Washington, DC 20005
Phone 202-408-2662
Fax 202-371-0181

INSURANCE, SECURITIES

Financial Executives Institute
10 Madison Avenue
P.O. Box 1938
Morristown, NJ 07962
Phone 973-898-4600
Fax 973-267-4031

Independent Insurance Agents of
America, Inc.
127 S. Peyton Street
Alexandria, VA 22314
Phone 703-683-4422
Fax 703-683-7556

National Association of Professional
Insurance Agents
400 North Washington Street
Alexandria, VA 22314
Phone 703-836-9340
Fax 703-836-1279

National Association of Realtors
430 North Michigan Avenue
Chicago, IL 60611
Phone 312-329-8200
Fax 312-329-8576

National Security Traders Association
One World Trade Center, #4511
New York, NY 10048
Phone 212-524-0484
Fax 212-321-3449

Securities Industry Association
120 Broadway, 35th Floor
New York, NY 10271
Phone 212-608-1500
Fax 212-608-1604

FEDERAL AND STATE EMPLOYEES

American Federation of Government
Employees
80 F Street, NW
Washington, DC 20001
Phone 202-737-8700
Fax 202-639-6441

American Federation of State, County,
and Municipal Employees
1625 L Street, NW
Washington, DC 20036
Phone 202-452-4800
Fax 202-429-1293

American Public Works Association
2345 Grand Boulevard, Suite 500
Kansas City, MO 64108
Phone 816-472-6100
Fax 816-472-1610

American Society for Public
Administration
1120 G Street NW, Suite 500
Washington, DC 20005
Phone 202-393-7878
Fax 202-638-4952

Federal Law Enforcement Officers
Association
P.O. Box 508
East Northport, NY 11731
Phone 516-368-6117
Fax 516-368-6429

Federal Managers Association
1641 Prince Street
Alexandria, VA 22314-2818
Phone 703-683-8700
Fax 703-683-8707

National Federation of Federal
Employees
1016 16th Street NW, Suite 300
Washington, DC 20036
Phone 202-862-4400
Fax 202-862-4432

FINANCE

American Bankers Association
1120 Connecticut Avenue, NW
Washington, DC 20039
Phone 202-663-5000
Fax 202-828-4547

Million Dollar Round Table
325 N. Touhy Avenue
Park Ridge, IL 60068
Phone 847-692-6378
Fax 847-518-8921

Mortgage Banker Association of
America
1125 15th Street, NW
Washington, DC 20005
Phone 202-861-6500
Fax 202-861-0734

American Finance Association
Blackwell Publishers
350 Main Street
Malden, MA 02148
Phone 800-835-6770
Fax 781-388-8232

HEALTH, ALLIED HEALTH

American Academy of Family
Physicians
8880 Ward Parkway
Kansas City, MO 64114
Phone 816-333-9700
Fax 816-822-0580

American Health Care Association
1201 L Street, NW
Washington, DC 20005
Phone 202-842-4444
Fax 202-842-3860

Health Physics Society
1313 Dolley Madison Boulevard,
Suite 402
McLean, VA 22101-3926
Phone 703-790-1745
Fax 703-790-2672

Healthcare Financial Management
Association
2 Westbrook Corporate Center,
Suite 700
Westchester, IL 60154
Phone 708-531-9600
Fax 708-531-0032

Medical Group Management Association
104 Inverness Terrace East
Englewood, CO 801121
Phone 303-799-1111
Fax 303-643-4427

National Health Lawyers Association
1120 Connecticut Avenue NW, Suite 950
Washington, DC 20036
Phone 202-833-1100
Fax 202-833-1105

LEISURE, TOURISM, TRAVEL

American Association for Leisure and
Recreation
1900 Association Drive
Reston, VA 22091
Phone 703-476-3400
Fax 703-476-9527

American Hotel and Motel Association
1201 New York Avenue NW, Suite 600
Washington, DC 20005
Phone 202-289-3100
Fax 202-289-3199

American Society of Travel Agents
1101 King Street, Suite 200
Alexandria, VA 22314
Phone 703-739-2782
Fax 703-684-8319

Travel and Tourism Research Association
546 East Main Street
Lexington, KY 40508
Phone 606-226-4344
Fax 606-226-4355

MANUFACTURING

Equipment and Tool Institute
1806 John's Drive
Glenview, IL 60025-1657
Phone 847-729-8550
Fax 847-729-3670

Chemical Manufacturers Association
1300 Wilson Boulevard
Arlington, VA 22209-2307
Phone 703-741-5000
Fax 703-741-6000

Industrial Fabrics Association
International
1801 County Road B W
Roseville, MN 55113-4061
Phone 612-222-2508
Fax 612-631-9334

National Association of Manufacturers
1331 Pennsylvania Avenue, NW
6th Floor, North Tower
Washington, DC 20004-1790
Phone 202-637-3000
Fax 202-637-3182

PROFESSIONAL SERVICES

American Bar Association
750 North Lake Shore Drive
Chicago, IL 60611-6281
Phone 312-998-5000
Fax 312-998-6281

American Institute of Certified Public
Accountants
1211 Avenue of the Americas
New York, NY 10036-8775
Phone 212-596-6200
Fax 212-596-6213

American Institute of Architects
1735 New York Avenue, NW
Washington, DC 20006-5292
Phone 202-626-7300
Fax 202-626-7420

Institute of Management
Consultants
521 5th Avenue, 35th Floor
New York, NY 10175-3598
Phone 212-697-8262
Fax 212-949-6571

National Society of Accountants
1010 North Fairfax Street
Alexandria, VA 22314-1574
Phone 703-549-6400
Fax 703-549-2984

Society of Women Engineers
120 Wall Street, 11th Floor
New York, NY 10005-3902
Phone 212-509-9577
Fax 212-509-0224

RETAILING

American Booksellers Association
828 South Broadway, Suite 625
Tarrytown, NY 10010-7000
Phone 212-645-2368
Fax 212-989-7542

Food Marketing Institute
800 Connecticut Avenue NW,
Suite 500
Washington, DC 20006-2709
Phone 202-452-8444
Fax 202-429-4519

National Home Furnishings
Association
P.O. Box 2396
High Point, NC 27261
Phone 910-883-1650
Fax 910-883-1195

National Restaurant Association
1200 17th Street, NW
Washington, DC 20036-3097
Phone 202-331-5900
Fax 202-331-2429

SMALL BUSINESSES

American Business Women's
Association
P.O. Box 8728
9100 Ward Parkway
Kansas City, MO 64114-0728
Phone 816-361-6621
Fax 816-361-4991

American Chamber of Commerce
Executives
4232 King Street
Alexandria, VA 22302-9950
Phone 703-998-0072
Fax 703-931-5624

National Federation of Independent
Business
600 Maryland Avenue SW, Suite 700
Washington, DC 20024
Phone 202-554-9000
Fax 202-554-0496

National Small Business United
1156 15th Street NW, Suite 1100
Washington, DC 20005
Phone 202-293-8830
Fax 202-872-8543

SUPERVISION, ADMINISTRATION, MANAGEMENT

American Management Association
1601 Broadway
New York, NY 10019-7420
Phone 212-586-8100
Fax 212-903-8168

American Society for Public
Administration
1120 G Street NW, Suite 700
Washington, DC 20005-3885
Phone 202-393-7878
Fax 202-638-4952

American Society of Association
Executives
1575 Eye Street, NW
Washington, DC 20005-1168
Phone 202-626-2723
Fax 202-371-8825

Human Resource Planning Society
317 Madison Avenue, Suite 1509
New York, NY 10017
Phone 212-490-6387
Fax 212-682-6851

National Management Association
2210 Arbor Boulevard
Dayton, OH 45439
Phone 937-294-0421
Fax 937-294-2374

Society for Human Resources
Management
1800 Duke Street
Alexandria, VA 22314-3499
Phone 703-548-3440
Fax 703-836-0367

United Fresh Fruit and Vegetable
Association
727 North Washington Street
Alexandria, VA 22314
Phone 703-836-3410
Fax 703-836-7745

American Wholesale Marketers
Association
1128 16th Street, NW
Washington, DC 20036-4808
Phone 202-463-2124
Fax 202-463-6456

WHOLESALERS

Automotive Warehouse Distributors
Association
9140 Ward Parkway, Suite 200
Kansas City, MO 64114
Phone 816-444-3500
Fax 816-444-0330

National Association of Wholesaler-
Distributors
1725 K Street NW, 3rd Floor
Washington, DC 20006
Phone 202-872-0885
Fax 202-785-0586

MAGAZINES AND JOURNALS

Association Management
American Society of Association
Executives
1575 I Street
Washington, DC 20005
Phone 202-626-2711
Fax 202-408-9635

Business and Society Review
Center for Business Ethics
350 Main Street
Waltham, MA 02148
781-891-2747

Business Marketing
740 N Rush Street
Chicago, IL 60611
Phone 312-649-5200
Fax 312-649-5462

Business Quarterly
Richard Ivey School of Business
London, Ontario, N6A 3K7
Canada
Phone 519-661-3309
Fax 519-661-3838

Business Week
McGraw-Hill, Inc.
1221 Avenue of the Americas, 39th
Floor
New York, NY 10020
Phone 212-512-2511

Canadian Manager
2175 Sheppard Avenue, E., #310
Willowdale, Ontario, M2J 1W8
Canada
Phone 416-493-0155
Fax 416-491-1670

Chief Executive
733 Third Avenue
New York, NY 10017
Phone 212-687-8288
Fax 212-687-8456

Financial Executive
10 Madison Avenue
Morristown, NJ 07960
Phone 973-898-4600
Fax 973-267-4031

Forbes
Forbes, Inc.
60 5th Avenue
New York, NY 10011
Phone 212-620-2200
Fax 212-206-5126

Fortune
Rockefeller Center
Time & Life Building
New York, NY 10020
Phone 212-522-1212
Fax 212-246-3375

Futurist
7910 Woodmont Avenue, Suite 450
Betheseda, MD 20814
Phone 301-656-8274
Fax 301-951-0394

Harvard Business Review
60 Harvard Way
Boston, MA 02163
Phone 617-495-6800
Fax 617-495-9933

Human Resource Planning
Human Resource Planning Society
317 Madison Avenue, Suite 1509
New York, NY 10017
Phone 212-490-6387
Fax 212-682-6851

Inc.
38 Commercial Wharf
Boston, MA 02110
Phone 617-248-8000
Fax 617-248-8090

Industrial Distribution
275 Washington Street
Newton, MA 02158-1646
Phone 617-964-3030
Fax 617-558-4327

Industrial Management
25 Technology Park / Atlanta
Norcross, GA 30092-2901
Phone 770-449-0461
Fax 770-263-8532

Journal of Accountancy
201 Plaza III
Harborside Financial Center
Jersey City, NJ 07311
Phone 201-938-3000
Fax 201-938-3329

Journal of Marketing
American Marketing Association
250 South Wacker Drive, Suite 200
Chicago, IL 60606
Phone 312-648-0536
Fax 312-648-4619

Journal of Property Management
National Association of Realtors
430 North Michigan Avenue
Chicago, IL 60611
Phone 312-329-6000
Fax 312-329-6039

Manage
National Management Association
2210 Arbor Boulevard
Dayton, OH 45439
Phone 937-294-0421
Fax 937-294-2374

Management Accounting
P.O. Box 433
Montvale, NJ 07645
Phone 201-573-9000
Fax 201-573-0639

Management Review
American Management Association
1601 Broadway
New York, NY 10019
Phone 212-586-8100
Fax 212-903-8083

Marketing News
250 South Wacker Drive
Chicago, IL 60606
Phone 312-993-9517
Fax 312-993-7540

Workforce
P.O. Box 2440
Costa Mesa, CA 92628-2440
Phone 714-751-1883
Fax 714-751-4106

Public Relations Quarterly
P.O. Box 311
Rhinebeck, NY 12572-0311
Phone 914-876-2081
Fax 914-876-2561

Sales and Marketing Management
355 Park Avenue S., 5th Floor
New York, NY 10010-1706
Phone 212-592-6300
Fax 212-592-6309

Sloan Management Review
77 Massachusetts Avenue
Cambridge, MA 02139-4307
Phone 617-253-7170
Fax 617-258-9739

Supervision
P.O. Box 1
Burlington, IA 52601-0001
Phone 319-752-5415
Fax 319-752-3421

Training Magazine
50 S. Ninth Street
Minneapolis, MN 55402-3118
Phone 612-333-0471
Fax 612-333-6526

Training & Development Journal
1630 Duke Street
Alexandria, VA 22314
Phone 703-683-8100
Fax 703-683-9203

NEWSLETTERS

Bottom Line/Tomorrow
Box 2614
55 Railroad Avenue
Greenwich, CT 06836-2614

Communication Briefings
1101 King Street, #110
Alexandria, VA 22314-2944

Communication at Work
Dartnell Corporation
747 Drescher Road #500
Horsham, PA 19044

First Line Supervisor
Dartnell Corporation
747 Drescher Road #500
Horsham, PA 19044

Productivity and Performance
Bureau of Business Practice, Inc.
24 Rope Ferry Road
Waterford, CT 06386

Sales and Marketing Executive
Dartnell Corporation
747 Drescher Road #500
Horsham, PA 19044

Supervisor for Technology &
Electronics Management
Bureau of Business Practice, Inc.
24 Rope Ferry Road
Waterford, CT 06386

A SAMPLING OF KEY DIRECTORIES

Associations Yellow Book
Monitor Publishing Company
104 Fifth Avenue, 2nd Floor
New York, NY 10010

Bacon's Magazine Directory
Bacon's Newspaper Directory
332 S. Michigan Avenue
Chicago, IL 60604

Business Control Atlas
American Map Corporation
46-35 54th Road
Maspeth, NY 11378

Community, Specialty & Free
Publications Yearbook
Editor and Publisher Company
11 W. 19th Street
New York, NY 10011

Directory of Conventions, Regional
Editions
Successful Meetings Databank
355 Park Avenue South
New York, NY 10010

Editor and Publisher Market Guide
Editor and Publisher Company
11 W. 19th Street
New York, NY 10011

Directory of Associations
Gales Research Inc.
835 Penobscot Building
Detroit, MI 48226-4094

Magazine Industry Marketplace
R.R. Bowker Company
12712 Dupont Circle
Tampa, FL 33626

Publisher's Yellow Pages
Morgan-Price Corporation
17782 Cowan Avenue, Suite D
Irvine, CA 92714

Standard Periodical Directory
Oxbridge Communications, Inc.
150 Fifth Avenue, Suite 302
New York, NY 10011

Tradeshow Week Data Book
121 Chanlon Road
New Providence, NJ 07974

Who's Who in the World
Marquis Who's Who
121 Chanlon Road
New Providence, NJ 07974

FOR FURTHER READING

Alessandra, Dr. Tony. *Charisma*. New York: Warner, 1998.

Alessandra, Dr. Tony. *The Platinum Rule*. New York: Warner, 1996.

Bedrosian, Margaret. *Speak Like a Pro*. New York: John Wiley & Sons, 1986.

Berns, Fred. *Sell Yourself! 501 Ways to Get Them to Buy from You*. Lafayette, CO: Power Promotions, 1998.

Boll, Carl. *Executives Jobs Unlimited*. New York: Macmillan, 1980.

Bright, Deborah. *Gearing Up for the Fast Lane: The Challenging of Exceptional Performance*. New York: Random House, 1986.

Burns, David. *Feeling Good: The New Mood Therapy*. New York: William Morrow, 1980.

Carnegie, Dale. *How to Win Friends and Influence People*, New York: Simon & Schuster, 1937.

Cathcart, Jim. *The Acorn Principle*. New York: St. Martin's, 1998.

Cohen, William A. *How to Make It Big as a Consultant*. New York: AMACOM Books, 1985.

Connelly, J. Campbell. *A Manager's Guide to Speaking and Listening*. New York: AMACOM Books, 1967.

Connor, Richard A., Jr., and Jeff Davidson. *Getting New Clients*, 2nd edition. New York: John Wiley & Sons, 1994.

Connor, Richard A., Jr., and Jeff Davidson. *Marketing Your Consulting and Professional Services*, 3rd edition. New York: John Wiley & Sons, 1997.

Davidson, Jeff. *The Complete Idiot's Guide to Assertiveness*. New York: Macmillan, 1997.

Davidson, Jeff. *The Complete Idiot's Guide to Reaching Your Goals*. New York: Macmillan, 1998.

Davidson, Jeff. *The Joy of Simple Living*. Emmaus, PA: Rodale, 1999.

Davidson, Jeff. *Marketing for the Home-Based Business*. Holbrook, MA: Adams Media, 1999.

Davis, Mitchell. *Talk Show Guest Directory.* Washington, DC: Broadcast Interview Source, 1999.

Dawson, Roger. *Roger Dawson's Secrets of Power Negotiating.* Franklin Lakes, NJ: Career Press, 1996.

Drucker, Peter. *The Effective Executive,* New York: Harper & Row, 1967.

Drucker, Peter. *The New Realities,* London: Heinemann, 1989.

Dubrin, Andrew J. *Winning at Office Politics.* New York: Ballantine Books, 1978.

Elsea, Dr. Janet. *First Impression, Best Impression.* New York: Simon & Schuster, 1986.

Engle, Peter H. *The Overachievers.* New York: Dial Press, 1976.

Kelley, Robert. *How to Be a Star at Work.* New York: Times Books, 1998.

Korda, Michael. *Power! How to Get It, How to Use It.* New York: Random House, 1975.

Kram, Kathy E. *Mentoring Processes at Work: Developmental Relationships in Managerial Careers.* Glenview, IL: Scott Foresman, 1985.

Lainson, Suzanne. *Crash Course.* New York: G.P. Putnam, 1985.

Machlowitz, Marilyn. *Success at an Early Age.* New York: Arbor House, 1984.

Maltz, Dr. Maxwell. *Psychocybernetics.* NY: Pocket Books, 1983.

Mandino, Og. *The Greatest Salesman in the World.* New York: Frederick Fell, 1968.

Maslow, Abraham. *Motivation and Personality,* New York: Harper & Row, 1954.

McCormack, Mark H. *What They Don't Teach You at Harvard Business School.* New York: Bantam Books, 1984.

Peale, Dr. Norman Vincent. *The Power of Positive Thinking.* New York: Walker, 1984.

Posner, Mitchell J. *Executive Essentials.* New York: Avon, 1982.

Ringer, Robert J. *Winning Through Intimidation.* Beverly Hills: L.A. Book Publishers, 1973.

Schatzki, Michael, and Wayne R. Coffey. *Negotiation: The Art of Getting What You Want.* New York: New American Library, 1981.

Welch, Mary Scott. *Networking.* New York: Warner Books, 1980.

Zey, Michael G. *Mentor Connection.* Chicago: Dow Jones-Irwin, 1984.

INDEX

ABOUT THE AUTHOR

J EFF DAVIDSON FREQUENTLY SPEAKS AT CONFERENCES, conventions, and executive retreats, and has made presentations to more than 500 groups in the U.S., Europe, and Asia on managing information and communication overload. Comments such as "Best of the convention," or "Best we've ever heard" represent typical feedback to Jeff's presentations.

Jeff is the author of 25 books, more than 3,000 articles, and numerous audio and videotape programs. His recent book, *The Joy of Simple Living* (Rodale), enjoyed a 50,000 first printing and was selected by two book clubs. Jeff's book, *Marketing for the Home-Based Business* (Adams Media), is one of the most popular in its field. Jeff's two-cassette album, *Get a Life* (Learn, Inc.), is a leading-edge program on living and working at a comfortable pace in a high-speed society.

His six-cassette album, *Simplifying Your Work and Your Life* (SkillPath), co-recorded with Dr. Tony Alessandra, gives career professionals the tools and practical information they need in the face of complexity in their everyday lives.

Jeff offers a blend of both keynote and seminar presentations on how to maintain balance while remaining profitable and competitive. His presentations include:

- How to Have More Breathing Space
- Choosing When It's Confusing
- Managing Multiple Priorities
- Relaxing at High Speed

Six of Jeff's speeches have been published in recent years in issues of the prestigious *Vital Speeches of the Day,* including *Relaxing at High Speed, Choosing When It's Confusing, Overworked or Overwhelmed?, Managing the Pace with Grace, World Population and Your Life,* and *Handling Information Overload.*

The *Washington Post,* where he's been featured eight times, called Jeff Davidson a "dynamo of business book writing."

Millions of people have read about Jeff in *USA Today, Los Angeles Times, San Francisco Chronicle,* and the *Chicago Tribune,* or have seen him featured on *Good Morning America, CBS Nightwatch, CNBC, Ask Washington,* and hundreds of regionally-based talk shows.

Jeff is one of a handful of distinguished authors who have had two or more of their books among "The Best Thirty Books of the Year" as selected by *Soundview Executive Book Summaries.* Other authors include Dr. Peter Drucker, Tom Peters, and Dr. Karl Albrecht. Cumulatively, Jeff's books have been selected by 20 major book clubs and published in 14 languages.

To inquire about Jeff's speaking availability, fax to 919-932-9982, send an e-mail to keynote@BreathingSpace.com, or visit http://www.JeffDavidson.com.